How To Get It Right When You Write

Book One
The Editing Process

Al Borowski, MEd, CSP

Pittsburgh, PA

How To Get It Right When You Write
Book One – The Editing Process

Library of Congress Catalog Number 00-105730

ISBN 0-9675335-0-3

> Borowski, Al
> How to get it right when you write:
> book one the editing process / by Al Borowski

Copyright © 2001 by Al Borowski, MEd, CSP. All rights reserved. No part of this book may be reproduced or transmitted in any form, or by any means electronic or mechanical, including photocopying, recording or by any information storage and retrieval system without written permission from the author, except for the inclusion of brief quotations in a review.

For inquiries or quantity purchases of this book, contact:

> Al Borowski, MEd, CSP
> Certified Speaking Professional
> Priority Communication Skills, Inc.
> P.O. Box 24505
> Pittsburgh, PA 15234
> Toll Free: 1-877-902-3314
> Fax: 412-561-7035
> E-mail: al@alborowski.com
> Website: www.alborowski.com

Editors:

Carol Baker Booth	Lin Fullem, MA	Pam Calore
Pittsburgh, PA	Fullem Associates	Pittsburgh, PA
	Uniontown, PA	

Cover Design: Diane Holleran
DL Graphics
Pittsburgh, PA

To my mother and father
I think they would have been proud.

Table of Contents

Acknowledgements   vii

Chapter One   **You Win — Guaranteed**

Seven Reasons Why You Should Read This Book 1
Will This Book Meet Your Objectives? 4
Action Plan 11

Chapter Two   **Fire! Ready! Aim!**

Five Things You Must Know Before You Write 13
Seven Helpful Hints 25
Yes, You Can 30
Subject - Verb - Relationship 41
Chapter Review 44

Chapter Three   **Mommy and Daddy Need To Party**

Five ways incorrect verbs and verb constructions destroy good writing
    Avoid Weak Verbs 47
    Avoid Passive Voice 67
    Avoid Nowhere Adverbs 80
    Avoid Artificial Antecedents 94
    Avoid Turning Strong Verbs into Nouns or Adjectives 110
Time Saving Bonus 117
    Using Grammar Checkers 117
    Using the Edit Capability 117
    Using Correct Words and Phrases 118
    Chapter Review 120

Chapter Four — Construction Signs That Mean Rough Road Ahead

Other constructions that destroy good writing
   Avoid Dang Modifiers 123
   Avoid Needless Words 125
   Avoid Clichés 130
   Avoid Jargon 132
   Avoid Incorrect Grammer 133
   Avoid Localisms 134
   Avoid Foreign Phrases 136
   Avoid Redundancy 137
   Avoid Polysyllabic Substitutions 139
   Avoid A Preponderance of Prepositional Phrases 145
   Avoid Weighted, Unnatural Language 146
   Avoid Weak Openings and Weak Closings 147
   Avoid The Gender Syndrome 157
   Avoid Negative Tone 158
   Avoid Abstract and Non-specific Terms 161
   Avoid Lack of Parallelism 162
   Avoid Confusing Abbreviations 166
   Chapter Review 169

Chapter Five — Reality Check

You Win — Guaranteed 181
Fire! Ready! Aim! 183
Mommy and Daddy Need to Party 185
Construction Signs That Mean Rough Road Ahead 189
Congratulations and Thank You 197

Acknowledgements

In my career, I have met thousands of very intelligent, talented, educated people who struggled with writing tasks. To them, and to anyone who struggles with business writing, I dedicate this book.

I also dedicate this book as a thank you to the many people who helped turn this book into reality.

I thank all my clients who trusted me with their employees, not once, but multiple times. Their confidence in me encouraged me to constantly update and refine the concepts you will find in this book. I truly appreciate all of you.

Next, I thank all the participants who attended my programs over the last 16 years. I thank you for attending and for suggesting ways to make this book more practical for everyone.

Thank you, Marylou, a wonderful wife, who never let me give up on this project. I thank you for your encouragement, your support, and constant re-focusing. Thank you for never giving up on me.

My daughter, Christine Marie Yanosick, was the glue that held this project together. Her infinite attention to detail, outstanding editing abilities, and dedication to this project, kept this project moving forward. Chrissie, as I affectionately call her, helped me stay focused on everything others needed from me to get this book to the production stage.

This book really started when my son, Brian, agreed to audio tape one of my two-day seminars. Then, Chrissie and my youngest daughter, Cathy Marie, transcribed the audio tapes and the project was on its way.

To Lin Fullem MA., Carol Baker Booth, and Pam Calore, who did a fantastic job of editing this book, I send special thanks. They helped me keep this book clear, concise, correct, conversational and complete. I loved the way they challenged me to practice what I preach.

Thank you, Diane Holleran, my graphics designer, for your patience and talent in translating the ideas in my head to a product I am truly proud of.

For checking the readability and practicality of this book, I thank Maureen Murray, Phillip Van Hooser, Susan Van Hooser and Kim Mercer. You were right on.

I also thank some wonderful, knowledgeable, giving professionals who shared their insights, experiences, and wisdom with me. I am very proud to be a member of the National Speakers Association (NSA) and the Pennsylvania Speakers Association. They generously gave me their time, friendship and their tips on writing, editing, publishing, marketing and promoting. I include in that thank you the Writers PEG (Professional Experts Group) of NSA. I thank them for constantly encouraging writers to publish.

Thank you, Nido Qubein, CSP, CPAE, Ed Scannell, CMP, CSP, Brian Tracy, CPAE, Ernie Emmerling and Dianne Wegley. You are ultimate professionals.

I thank my sister, Mary Bau, D.Ed. She motivated me to direct this book to a much broader base of readers.

And finally, I thank you, the readers who bought the book. When you finish the book, please tear out the Comments Form in the back of the book, jot down your comments and fax them back to me. Your comments will help make future editions of the book more valuable to others.

Chapter One
You Win – Guaranteed

Seven Reasons Why You Should Read This Book

Reason # 1 **This book works - Guaranteed.**

This book contains ideas and techniques that work – guaranteed. Most people write a book and then go on tour with their books. I have done just the opposite. I have spent 14 years conducting business writing workshops across the United States and Canada with people who have shared their frustrations, fears, doubts, and problems with business writing.

If you are not happy with this book for any reason, return it to me and I will be delighted to return your money. If you are not happy with the book, you lose and I lose.

Reason # 2 **You will learn these techniques easily and apply them immediately.**

Some of these techniques you already know but haven't applied to your business writing. Some of them you have accessible in your computer and may not know about them. Or, you may have known about them and have not learned how to use them. Some of them completely contradict what you learned in school.

Therefore, you spent your business career deprived of tools that could have improved your corporate image and income.

Reason # 3 **You will gain a personal business-writing coach.**

This book creates a partnership. You and I must go through this book together if you plan to improve your writing skills. As we progress through the pages, I will ask you to circle words or phrases, draw lines through them or read them out loud. This will simulate the experience of participating in one of my writing workshops.

As part of this partnership, I become your personal coach. I invite you to contact me. If you don't understand clearly what I have written, or, if you want more information, let me know. Call me; write me; fax me; e-mail me.

If you disagree with anything I suggest or write, call me; write me; fax me; e-mail me. If you find errors or inconsistencies in this book, call me; write me; fax me. I said this book creates a partnership. I mean it.

Al Borowski, MEd, CSP
Priority Communication Skills, Inc.
P.O. Box 24505
Pittsburgh, PA 15234
Office: 412-561-7628
Toll Free: 1-877-902-3314
Fax: 412-561-7035
E-mail: al@alborowski.com
www.alborowski.com

Reason # 4 **You will learn the reasons *why* these techniques work and how they will improve your writing, your attitude and your income.**

Unlike most books on writing, this book tells you *why*.

In my business writing seminars and workshops, I tell the participants that I'm a **Whys Guy**. I use this phrase to get their attention and then explain that I like to ask the question *Why*. If I suggest something, I like to offer reasons *why* I suggest them. If you understand *why* you should or should not do something, you accept it more readily and benefit from it much more.

My purpose is not to change your writing style. I don't want to change your style. I don't know how to change your style. I don't have the right to change your style. Nor does anyone else! They may have the right and responsibility to add, subtract or change information. They may eliminate company sensitive information or add facts you might not be aware of. They may correct your spelling, punctuation or grammar, but they do not have the right to change your writing style. Your writing style is **your** writing style. It's like the smile on your face. It belongs to you.

So, if I suggest a technique or recommend you eliminate one of your writing habits, I will offer you several reasons *why* you should. For example, in Chapter Four's, "**Weak Openings and Weak Closings,**" I will tell you to avoid the phrase "***Per your request***." I will also offer you at least five reasons *why* you should.

Reason # 5 **You will practice what you learn and get immediate feedback to check your progress.**

With many lessons in this book, you will find practice exercises. After the exercises, I offer suggestions on several approaches to the activities. You will find that, in business writing, you have alternatives. Those alternatives are based on certain factors which you will learn throughout the book. This means you can still use your creativity while performing a business function.

Reason # 6 **You will learn from real-life business situations and writing samples.**

Fourteen years of conducting public and in-house seminars and workshops have allowed me to review thousands of business writing documents. The sample sentences you will see in this book represent the types of writing I have seen. The samples are not direct lifts from original samples I evaluate as part of my on-site workshops. I have changed the sentences around to illustrate the specific writing problems people face. Some of you reading this book might say to yourself, "Gee, he's read my memos." Believe me, the sentences in this book show common errors all of us commit.

Reason # 7 **You will find this book easy to read and apply.**

I have tried to practice what I preach in this book. I wrote this book in a conversational tone so that you would feel you were sitting in one of my workshops.

Play *make believe*. Pretend you are in the workshop with twenty other people who will stimulate and support you through the program. Complete the pencil and paper activities as if you were actively involved in a workshop.

Talk to yourself, or me, or the book as you work through the pages or the exercises. This will add an auditory dimension to your learning process and will help you remember some techniques we will cover. You will see, hear, and experience positive changes as you apply the ideas in this book.

Will This Book Meet Your Objectives?

The next section will help you decide where this book will help you. It allows you to mark the objectives you want to achieve. Each objective carries an introductory description. After you have read the description, place a check mark in the box next to objective you want to achieve. If you check enough boxes to make the journey through this book worth your time and effort, great.

If not, great. Put it back on the shelf. If you already bought the book and now decide it's not worth anything to you, terrific. Send the book back to me and I'll refund your money. I want you to be completely delighted with this book. If this book works for you, I hope you will recommend it to your friends.

If you decide to continue reading this book, you can use those check marks to create an action plan for improving your writing.

Yes, I Want To

❏   **Save time**

That is the main reason I wrote this book. I constantly meet intelligent, highly skilled people who spend entirely too much time on their business writing tasks. For some of you, I will cut in half the time you spend on writing. If you save 10%, 15%, or 20%, you're still ahead of the game. Let me give you one idea on how I can save you that time.

Most of you can relate to the two-page letter that should be a one-page letter. I am going to show you *why* people tend to write two-page letters, and how quickly, easily and painlessly you can turn a two-page letter into a one-page letter. First, you will learn how to cut your two-page letters to one-page through powerful and easy-to-learn editing techniques. Then, you will learn techniques to consistently write one-page letters from the start.

❏ **Get better results**

Too many people waste too much time, money, ink, trees, paper and effort on letters, memos, e-mails and reports that get no results. Sometimes, those documents never get read. If they are not read, they definitely cannot get results. In this book, you will see some reasons why people do not read what they receive.

Also, you will learn some helpful hints on how to increase the chances your writing gets read. That increases your chances of achieving the results you want.

❏ **Become clear and concise**

Some people think more is better. In business writing, less is better. Less gets you better results. This book will show you specific editing techniques to cut excess from your writing. More specifically, you will learn *why* those techniques are important and *why* they work.

I always tie the words clear and concise together in my writing seminars. Sometimes you must sacrifice conciseness to be clear. As you go through this book, you will see specific examples of where and how you could and should sacrifice conciseness for clearness.

❏ **Set the proper tone**

If you set a negative tone, you may never get the results

you are looking for. The first five words of a letter can dictate the tone of a letter. That's true - the first five words! Suppose you get home tonight and in the mailbox you find an envelope. You open the envelope and the first five words of that letter say, "We regret to inform you." Are you now a "happy camper?"

Immediately, that letter creates a negative attitude. Chances are pretty high that the person who wrote the letter will not realize the benefits of a well-written, positive letter.

Also, think about the meaning of those words. Do you really think the people that write those letters "regret to inform you?" I doubt it.

❏ **Make more money**

This may prove the most important reason for you using this book. Please remember the focus of this book is business writing, not creative writing. I am not going to show you how to make more money by selling your great American novel, your hit Broadway play or your book of poetry. I am going to show you how to make your business writing more valuable which makes you more valuable.

The better you can communicate, particularly on paper, the better your chances for promotion. Think for a moment of the power you possess. Think of your business writing in these terms. *People decide important business issues based on what you write.*

That's really the only reason you write in the business world - to inform people well enough that they buy into your idea, your product, your project, your service, or your message. That gives you a lot of responsibility and a lot of power.

The more you can save people time and can get results for them, the more valuable you become.

❏ **Improve my personal and corporate image**

Remember, people decide important business issues based

on what you write. If you can save those people time, if you can get results for your audience, that makes you unbelievably important. If you take the time, effort and dedication to follow the suggestions and techniques in this book, you will increase the chances of becoming a better, more-rewarded writer.

❑ **Eliminate fear and dread of writing**

Fear and dread are two words that come up in most of my writing seminars and workshops. That's how most people look at business writing. They wake up in the morning and say, "Shall I go to the office and write that letter or call the assisted-death doctor?" Those are the only two options they face every morning.

I am going to show you why people fear and dread writing and how quickly, easily, and painlessly you can turn writing into an exciting activity. If you save time, get results, improve your image, and make more money, I think that's exciting.

❑ **Reduce stress and frustration**

This benefit pertains particularly to managers and supervisors who must review the writings of the people who work for them. This situation often turns into a stressful and frustrating experience. Let me explain.

Pretend that Cathy works for me. She gives me something she has written and asks me to review it. After checking it, I say to her, "Cathy, you're doing a good job. The problem is that this doesn't have the 'oooommf' or the 'pizazz' I'm looking for. Try it again."

Cathy is frustrated because she has no idea what I'm talking about or looking for. I'm frustrated because I cannot, in clear, specific language, explain to her what I want. I know what it is when I see it, but I cannot detail what I think is wrong with her writing or how to correct it.

This book will show you specific, graphic, tested ways to

turn a negative, stressful and frustrating situation into a positive, constructive and rewarding experience.

❏ **Make my readers think I am brilliant**

Successful writing means making your readers believe you are writing to them and them alone. If this objective was not one you shared when you first picked up this book, I hope to influence you to adopt it for your own.

Too much business writing today sounds like it comes straight from a robot, straight from an android, straight from a machine. The writing has no warmth, no character, no personality and very little reality. People want to know that you are a real person. They want to be treated like people, not numbers or bits and bytes that have importance only to the computer. They want to be written to, not at.

No matter what company or organization you work for, you are in the people business. If you are for-profit, you make that profit from people. If you are non-profit, not-for-profit or a government agency, you are in business to serve people. I will show you how, when and where to become more personal with your business writing. That is how you increase your chances of getting results.

❏ **Focus on my audience**

The easiest way to increase your chances of success with your business writing is to focus on your audience. This book will show you several ways to appeal to your audience, whether you write to a technical or non-technical audience. Also, you will learn the reasons why this offers you the best chances at success.

❏ **Check my writing for quality**

In this book, you will find manual and electronic ways to test the quality of your writing based on its readability. These measurements of structure, grammar, spelling, and clarity help you speed up the process of sending a well-written, audience-focused document to your readers.

❑ **Flush out "fony frazes"**

Some of you reading this book already know some favorite *fony frazes* you want to eliminate. Others may not know that some phrases we will discuss actually weaken writing. Not only will I list the phrases, I will explain *why* and *how* they destroy good writing. I will also share with you what you can substitute for those phrases.

For example, you will learn five reasons *why* you should never use the phrase *per your request* in your business writing.

❑ **Build confidence in my writing**

Many people who attend my writing workshops show great courage telling me they lack confidence in their writing. I assure the attendees that most of them already have the confidence they need.

I am willing to bet that 90% of the time when you write a letter, memo or report, you already know what information you want to appear in that document. That information already resides in your brain. Most of your writing deals with information you are familiar with. If you believe that, then 90% of the work is done.

The problem comes when you transfer that information from your brain to the paper. That's where this book becomes a valuable tool for you. It will show you how to build a bridge from your brain to your keyboard to match the ideas in your head to the words that appear on paper.

❑ **Write in a conversational manner**

Yes, you should write the way you talk. I will show you why; I will show you how; I will show you when. To put your mind at ease and to calm the academics who might read this book, let me say this. Write the way you speak; then edit, edit, edit to achieve your goals. You will see more on how to use this technique later.

❏ **Create exciting writing**

Your goal in business writing is not to create the great American novel. Business writing differs greatly from the *creative* writing you did in school. However, I will show you several techniques novelists and journalists use to get their readers interested.

More importantly, once you see the success you have with your writing, the more excited you will become. Getting desired results from your writing can become a powerful drug. I will show you how to get ***high*** on your writing.

You Win - Guaranteed

Action Plan

As I read this book, I will focus on ways to:
- ❏ Save time
- ❏ Get better results
- ❏ Become clear and concise
- ❏ Set the proper tone
- ❏ Make more money
- ❏ Improve my personal and corporate image
- ❏ Eliminate the fear and dread of writing
- ❏ Reduce stress and frustration
- ❏ Make my readers think I'm brilliant
- ❏ Focus on my audience
- ❏ Check my writing for quality
- ❏ Flush out "fony frazes"
- ❏ Build confidence in my writing
- ❏ Write in a conversational manner
- ❏ Create exciting writing

"Too many people waste too much time, money, ink, trees, paper and effort on letters, memos, e-mails, and reports that get no results."

Chapter Two
Fire! Ready! Aim!

The fastest and easiest way to save time and get better results with your writing is to know and understand a few basic concepts *before* you start to write.

Five Things You Must Know Before You Write

1. *"Your business writing is a valuable corporate asset."*

   People decide important business issues based on what you write.

   Think about that. That's why you write. Your image, your organization's image, and thus, your income depend on how well you can communicate business ideas. You might be the smartest person on the planet. You might have the best ideas, solutions, or product concepts, but if you cannot communicate them clearly and effectively to others, you may not progress as far as you would like in the corporate world. Or, you may not impact the world as you might be able to.

   This is particularly true with your business writing. Your readers do not have the ability to ask you questions, study your body language, or read your mind when they read your documents. But, your clear, concise, correct, complete, and conversational business writing allows your audience to save time and get better results. That makes you extremely valuable and important.

   This book will show you specific, tested and graphic ways for you to create business writing that saves you time and increases the chances for you to get better results.

2. *The biggest time waster in business writing is spending too much time writing.*

   To understand the biggest time waster in business writing, you must first recall something I feel you already know.

   Good writing requires at least four stages. Those stages are: **Prewriting,**

Writing, Editing, and Proofreading. Some authors consider rewriting another stage. I prefer to use the terms editing and rewriting interchangeably. As we progress through the book, you will see why.

Most people spend most of their time in the writing stage. Informal surveys of my writing workshop participants tell me this. That practice wastes time and effort. In reality, you should spend the *least* amount of time in the writing stage. I know you feel like I've lost my mind. But again, I will prove that to you and show you how to accomplish that piece of magic.

Also, you will find the writing stage to be the easiest to complete. I know that sounds crazy and contrary to all conventional wisdom and the nasty feelings inside your heart and head. In the companion book, ***How To Get It Right When You Write – Book Two – The Writing Process***, I will prove that to you.

Let me explain why you should spend the least amount of time in the writing stage. Can you recall a term paper you wrote with the hopes of getting a good grade?

Where did you spend most of your time with that project? If you cared about that grade, you probably spent most of your time in the library compiling the research. You spent endless hours taking notes on 3"x5" or 5"x8" cards, a letter or legal pad or dropping coins or feeding plastic cards into the copy machine. With all this data gathered, you probably spent a Saturday or Sunday afternoon with all that information scattered in neat piles on your dining room table or living room floor.

Then, you carefully crafted your masterpiece of practical plagiarism. We've all been through the drill.

To summarize the analogy, you spent most of your time in the **Prewriting** stage gathering, organizing, selecting, eliminating and ranking your information. The actual writing took significantly less time. After you wrote the paper, you probably gave it to a family member to proofread before handing it in.

Indeed, you should spend more time in the **Prewriting** stage than the **Writing Stage**.

And, you should spend more time in the **Editing Stage** than the **Writing Stage**.

This book focuses on the **Editing Process**. It will show you how to work with documents you have created and how to improve them.

The companion book to this book, ***How To Get It Right When You Write – Book Two – The Writing Process*** details all the steps, activities and information you need to focus on before you start to write.

3. *You can eliminate your fear and dread of writing by knowing its source.*

Let me share with you several reasons why many people fear and dread business writing. To do that, please join me in a mental time capsule that takes us back in time – back to the fifth and sixth grades. I realize that is quite a trip for some of us, but, come with me.

Back in the fifth and sixth grades, you probably went through the school system similar to the way I did. You spent all day with the same person; it wasn't your mother or father. You spent a big part of your day with your elementary school teacher. I admire elementary school teachers. They are my heroes. They face a lot of challenges. They have to teach you science, math, social studies, English, and geography. They sometimes concerned themselves with eraser clapping, milk money, and PTA meetings. One of these responsibilities is to teach you English. When they put on their English teachers' hats, their primary responsibility was to teach you the concept of *a sentence*.

Back in fifth and sixth grade, we were young. We were impressionable. And, coming from authority figures we heard words like ***declarative, interrogative, exclamatory, imperative***. Terrifying sounding words, right? How many of you use those words on a daily basis? That's what I figured.

That experience with those four terrifying words left an impression on us – **Big People Like Big Words**. What other conclusion could we come to? Our knowledge base was very limited. We didn't know any better. We were young and very impressionable.

Not only did those teachers use those four big words on us to define the kinds of sentences, they reinforced our false impressions by teaching us the types of sentences. In the fifth and sixth grades, we saw the following:

This is a simple sentence.

This is a compound sentence; it contains two independent clauses.

This is a complex sentence which contains one dependent and one independent clause.

This is a compound-complex sentence and because it contains two independent clauses and a dependent clause, it becomes a long sentence.

In our young, impressionable minds, what then became the standard by which we thought we were going to be judged? Long sentences! First, we learned that **Big People Like Big Words**. Now, we learn that **Big People Like Big Sentences.**

Those elementary school teachers took a very logical approach. They started very simply and ended with more difficult material. This approach showed us the various ways we speak and the various types of sentences we could use in writing. Unfortunately, in our young, impressionable minds, we retained only the message:

Big People Like Big Words – Big People Like Big Sentences

Then, you entered the seventh grade. Maybe by this time, you met a specialist - a dedicated English teacher. That dedicated English teacher assumed that the fifth and sixth grade teachers taught you all these neat things about sentences. Now you have to put these sentences together into something called a "paragraph."

Think about your first encounter with paragraph writing. I know the only two things you ever really remember about paragraph writing. I know those things because I ask participants in my workshops, "What do you remember about writing that first paragraph?" I get eight to ten different answers. Number one and number two are always the same.

Think back to that first paragraph you had to write. Tell me what you remember about that first paragraph. **(Remember, I asked you to play make believe.)** Go ahead, say it out loud. Or, if you're reading this in your office or on a plane, and you don't want people to throw a net over your head, say it to yourself. Tell me the first thing you remember about writing that first paragraph. Agony! Okay, what else? Say it; I know it's on the tip of your tongue.

Yes, that's right, **Indent**. That's number one on the hit parade - **Indent**. Of all of the things that people could remember about writing, what sticks in their brains? **Indent**! Now, many letters we receive come to us left justified, which means many people have dropped the concept of indenting.

The second thing people tell me they remember about writing their first paragraph is that that first paragraph had to be 100 words. Either 100 words or a certain number of sentences. Remember how we used to write? We looked at that blank sheet and uttered the writer's prayer, "Please God, let words appear." We wrote that first sentence and then we counted the words. "12 - yes! We're on our way."

Then we looked for the second sentence and wrote that down. Then what did we do? We counted the words. Did we start with the second sentence? No, we went back to the first. Maybe it grew while we were looking for the second one. We associated writing with a number.

Then, we entered the tenth grade, eleventh grade, or twelfth grade. What kind of writing are we doing now? Remember those dreaded assignments — term papers, themes, compositions, book reports? We are no longer talking 100 words. Now we're talking ten pages! Remember how suddenly the margins got bigger? Remember this stuff? We learned how to play the game. Remember how our penmanship improved? We used to write small. Ten pages, wow! All of a sudden, our writing became larger. That's how we got to 10 pages.

Also, back then, when we had to write that 10-page term paper, we introduced ourselves to two items – a dictionary and a thesaurus. And, we started doing bizarre things – like utilizing "utilize" rather than using "use." We wrote the paper and it was only eight pages long. That will never do. So we reread the paper and found this little word "use." That word was too small. So, we looked in the dictionary and found the word "utilize" – the stuff dreams are made of.

Early in our education, we learned some valuable lessons. First, **big**

words fill pages. What was our objective? We had to fill pages. Second, we learned a system for good grades. The more big words we used, the better our grade. The better the grades, the more big words we used. Writing became a game. We knew how to play the game. That stuck with us.

In the fifth and sixth grade, we heard words like *declarative* and *interrogative*. When we wrote our term papers, we used words like *utilize* and *endeavor*.

Then some of us entered college. Many college students still remember the horror of blue books during the final exam. Did those blue books tell what you knew about the subject? No! Did they tell how you could apply that information? No! All that experience told was how well you could fill a blue book.

Throughout your formal education, you had a number associated with writing, **100 Words - 10 Pages - 2 Blue Books**.

Now you get into a business environment to find out that none of that stuff works. It's a completely different focus.

Because we focused on getting to **100 Words - 10 Pages - 2 Blue Books**, the length of our sentences increased, our words got bigger, and we used more prepositional phrases. Because we wrote like that in school, we naturally transferred that approach to business writing.

In business, our audience does not have time to read two pages when one page will do. Our audience is not impressed by the length of our sentences or the extent of our vocabulary.

In this book, we're looking to save time. We're looking to get different results. We're not trying to impress people.

We have to decide important business issues to get business results. That's what we're going to focus on in this book. We will focus on how to take the information you know, and build a bridge from your brain to the paper or keyboard to *help others decide important business issues*.

To get better results with our business writing, we need to reverse that process. We need to become clear, concise, correct, complete, and conversational.

This book will share specific, tested, graphic ways to achieve that in the **Editing Process**.

4. ***To become a better writer, you must understand the communication process.***

Why do we write? The obvious answer is – to communicate.

Many of you have probably learned that in communication you have a sender, a receiver, and feedback. Those are the components of communication, but that does not tell us what communication **is**. Let's build an idea of what communication is from some of the answers my workshop attendees offer.

When I ask people what communication is, here is one answer I hear. "Communication is the dissemination of information." What do you think? Yuk! Another definition I get is that "Communication is the transfer of ideas." Buy that? I don't. I also get this answer. "Communication is the exchange of information." Still not close.

Remember, I asked you to pretend you are participating in one of my business writing workshops as you read this book. Let's pretend that two weeks ago, I sent each of you a letter after you signed up for one of my workshops. The first line of that letter said, "When you come to the workshop, please bring a paradigm of communication with you."

Trust me. I did not use the word "paradigm" to impress you. But think about that. I sent you a letter and the first sentence asked you to bring a "paradigm" of communication. The word "paradigm" in that context helps me prove two points.

First, far too many people who attend my workshops do not know or are not sure what that word means. Second, those who know what it means may use the word to impress others who do not know what it means.

Pretend for a moment that you do not know what the word means. When you read that first sentence of my letter asking you to bring a "paradigm," you will do one of four things. The first thing you might do is throw it away. In your mind you would say to yourself, "Who is this clown trying to impress?" If you throw away the letter, I failed to get the **results** I was looking for.

If you don't throw the letter away, the second thing you might do is **assume**. You would assume that reading the rest of the letter would explain what the word "paradigm" meant. Or, you would assume that the word carried little value and that the remainder of the letter would explain the important information.

The third thing you might do is ask the next twelve people who walk by your desk, "What's a paradigm?" They don't know either! That wastes time. Our goal is to save time. We want to save time for you and your readers.

So, finally in total frustration, you resort to the last resort. You look up the word in the dictionary. You then read the dictionary definition, reread my letter, check the dictionary definition one more time to see if I used it properly, and you say to yourself, "I'm going to fix his wagon." So, you write me a letter and you say, "We don't have any **paradigms** around here, but we have a lot of **affamits**."

I have no idea what an **affamit** is. Check out what just happened.

We have just disseminated information. We have just transferred ideas. We have just exchanged information. Has communication taken place? Not even close. As far as I know, affamits don't exist. We do have a thing called a **paradigm**. Before I tell you what a paradigm is, let me tell you what communication is.

The word communication comes from a Latin word that means "to share." Before you share something with someone, one other condition exists. You must care. You must care that the reader understands what you've said. You don't have to like the person; you don't have to agree with the person to communicate.

If I looked at Galina and said, "Galina, this is the best writing program you'll ever attend." Galina looks at me and says, "Borowski, you're full of canal water." Are we communicating? Sure we are. You don't have to like the person or agree with the person.

She understands what I'm saying and I understand what she's saying.

Fire! Ready! Aim!

At least, we are communicating. **Communication simply means caring enough to ensure people understand your words the same way you do.**

Now that you know and understand what communication is, let me tell you what a "paradigm" is. A paradigm is a pattern, a model or an example by which you are supposed to learn something. Some of you might remember when your fifth grade teacher taught you:

I am	We are
You are	You are
He, she or it is	They are

Or, you might remember comparison of adjectives:

Good, better, best

Small, smaller, smallest

Those are paradigms. They are patterns, models or examples by which you are supposed to learn something.

We communicate in only two ways – verbally and nonverbally. The word "verbal" means written and spoken. A lot of people think the word "verbal" only means spoken. That's not true. The word "verbal" means written and spoken.

The verbal part includes the words you use and the tone you project with your words. If people do not understand those words, that communication will go nowhere. If your readers understand those words, then the **tone** you use – how you say it – becomes more important than the **words.**

When I go home at night and I say to my wife, "Marylou, what's the matter?" and in a soft, almost inaudible tone, with head pitched downward she says, "Nothing." Do I believe her? No way! The word was "nothing." How she said it was even more important.

"Marylou, what's the matter?" She snarls in a loud, defiant tone, **"NOTHING!"** Then I know I'm the cause.

How To Get It Right When You Write

"It's not what you say. It's how you say it." Remember that old expression? It's true.

The nonverbal signals we send with our body language reveal much more than the actual words we use. When we slam doors with frowns on our faces and let out exasperated sighs of disgust, we are letting people know we are not happy. We don't say a word, but people get the message.

Another example of nonverbal signals is eye contact. Have you ever walked into someone's office and said "Hey Al, I've got a great idea." Al responds in a low, monotone, pestered-sounding voice, "Yeah, go ahead, tell me about it." And, Al never looks at you. He continues looking down at the pile of papers he was working on.

Or, he gets up from the desk by placing both hands flat on the desk to push himself up. Once he's up, he folds his arms behind his back.

Then he starts pacing. While he paces, he checks the floor, checks the ceiling tiles, looks out the window to see if anyone stole his car, and finally checks his watch to make sure he brought it with him. All this while, he never looks at you. Does that mean he's not listening? No! He hears every word you say. How does that make you feel? Right! About one inch tall.

What is communication? Communication is *caring* and *sharing*. Do you get the feeling Al cares about you? He is showing you that he cares about himself, not you. He is not sharing any of himself with you.

Volumes of evidence show how nonverbals affect communication. For this book, let's focus on how the nonverbals affect your writing.

When you write a letter, memo, report or proposal, do you have the benefit of these nonverbal signals? No. We've wiped out more than half your ability to communicate.

Now do you understand why writing becomes so difficult? We have grown accustomed to communicating by using the nonverbals of our body language. We become frustrated when we cannot communicate as effectively on paper.

This is also why you would prefer to talk to someone, rather than write them a memo or letter. In speech, you have the benefit of reading that person's nonverbals or having them read yours. In writing, we must rely on words and tone. That's it, **words** and **tone**.

You do have some nonverbals. If you wrote an important letter to a customer in pencil, wrinkled it while putting it in the envelope, spilled coffee on it while you were writing it, misspelled the person's name, and sent it four weeks late, I think that's nonverbal.

For the most part, when you write, you do not have the benefit of nonverbal signals. That's why writing is so tough. We can only rely on the words and the tone when writing. That's one reason why people *fear and dread* writing. And that's why they are not getting positive results. They are taking a negative attitude toward writing. They know something's wrong, but they don't know how to overcome it.

This book will show you how to take all the objectives you checked in the beginning of the book and use them as building blocks to better writing.

5. *Speed Traps can slow you down.*

   Another thing that affects you every time you write is something I call **Speed Traps**.

   The Speed Traps are:
   - Think speed
   - See speed
   - Read speed
   - Speak speed
   - Write speed

   This means we think faster than we see; we see faster than we read; we read faster than we speak, and we speak faster than we write.

   Stuck between your ears is a marvelous computer. That computer processes information at the rate of at least 480 words a minute. Every minute of the day you are processing information. Most of you move along at 600, 800, 1000, 2000, maybe 3000 words a minute. That's a lot of processing capability.

And, you do this thinking whether you're awake or asleep. Did you ever wake up in the middle of the night with the feeling you were falling off a building or out of bed? Have you ever gotten up in the middle of the night with a solution to a problem? That's because we are always processing information.

At the speak speed, normal conversational speech ranges between 125 and 250 words a minute. That's normally how fast people can talk. Let's consider how fast people can write or type.

For the purposes of this book, let's assume that each of you reading this book can write or type 100 words a minute. Few people can do that. If you can, I applaud you. Most people cannot.

Think about what that means. In your head, you can process 480 words a minute. With your fingers, you can only write or type 100 words a minute. That's why writing is so tough for some people. We think faster than we can type or write. Human nature has created a bottleneck.

Have you ever had that situation where you had a project to complete, you had all those great ideas, you were really excited, and you sat at the keyboard to type? What happened? They're gone. All those great ideas seem to disappear.

The good news is that once information enters your brain, it never leaves. You may forget what compartment you put it in, but it never leaves your brain. I'm going to show you some ways to overcome this.

Before I do, let's take the speed trap problem one level lower. Although you process 480 words a minute, not all 480 words pertain to the subject you are writing about. Perhaps only 25 or 50 words are the maximum number of words or ideas from that string of 480 going through your head that pertain to your subject. That creates another bottleneck.

Even further, those 25 or 50 words are not stored in one neat little box inside your head. They're scattered throughout your brain. So, the first task you face when you write is pulling all those ideas together into one package to refer to as you write.

Let's review what all this means. You are capable of thinking 480 words a minute. All 480 words do not pertain to the subject of your writing task. Perhaps 25 to 50 of those words really relate.

Many people try to write using a process I call *mental outlining*. This means that rather than writing those thoughts down on paper or in their computers, they just start writing.

Please understand that if you try to write by using a *mental outline*, you compete with everything else going on in your business and personal life. That's what is stored in your brain – your business and personal life. That's a lot of competition! That mental competition is another reason why some people struggle with their business writing.

Seven Helpful Hints

To help you understand and remember some of the other concepts you will find in this book, I will now share some helpful hints with you.

Helpful Hint # 1 *Write to be understood, not to overwhelm.*

Your goal in business writing should be to inform people. This means you need to express ideas in a fashion they can read quickly, understand, remember, and act upon.

Remember when I used the word *paradigm*? I told you my goal was not to impress you. I'm sure each of you have met bosses and coworkers who love to throw around big words. Their goal clearly is to impress someone, or, even worse, to demean them.

Let's put that another way. **Keep your business writing conversational.** Your business writing should sound as natural as a telephone conversation. That's all business writing is - conversation on paper.

Remember, in your job, you are in a people-to-people business. I seriously doubt whether any of you start a conversation with a friend, coworker, boss or client, *per your request*. At least I hope you don't. Keep your writing as natural and as personal as a telephone conversation.

In his book, *Talking Straight,* Lee Iacocca wrote, **"Write the way you talk. If you don't talk that way, don't write that way."** Thank you, Mr. Iacocca. You just summed up my book in two sentences.

For those purists in the group, I will add a side bar to Mr. Iacocca's sound advice. **Write the way you speak; then, edit, edit, edit.** Check your first draft to ensure you have used complete sentences and correct spelling, punctuation and grammar.

Remember, this book is not a business writing document. Please recognize that I intend this book to look and sound like a workshop. For that reason, you will see incomplete sentences, strange phrases and spellings. That is on purpose to simulate the conversational, highly interactive way I conduct my workshops.

Helpful Hint # 2 *Become intimate with your grammar checkers.*

This is another way of saying always leave time to edit and possibly to rewrite your first draft. Someone once said, "There's no such thing as good writing, just good rewriting."

I realize in the hectic business world, finding time for editing and rewriting becomes a challenge. However, investing the time to run your writing through grammar checkers pays huge dividends.

Many of the latest versions of word processors already come equipped with grammar checkers. If yours does not, you might want to consider investing $49.00 in a computer program that will definitely help save you time, improve the quality of your writing, and eliminate the embarrassment of misspelled words, incorrect grammar or confusing writing styles.

Throughout this book I will refer to these grammar checkers and show you why some people hesitate to use them. I will show you how you can use them to your benefit.

Helpful Hint # 3 *Average 18 words per sentence.*

The important word in this helpful hint is "average." That does not mean every sentence must be 18 words long.

I tell my participants in my business writing workshops that I would bet them $10.00 that their average is 20 - 24 words. If they are technically oriented, government oriented, legally oriented, or academically oriented, that average shoots upwards to the 28 - 30 word average.

Fire! Ready! Aim!

You've already learned why most people write long sentences - **100 Words - 10 Pages - 2 Blue Books. Big People Like Big Words - Big People Like Big Sentences**. Using shorter sentences will help your readers read your writing faster, understand it easier and remember it better. As we progress through this book, you will see how to quickly, easily, and painlessly turn long sentences into clear and concise writing.

I feel confident most of you have heard the expression, "in 25 words or less…"

"In 25 words or less, tell us why we should send you to Hawaii."

Please understand the importance of this concept. Do you understand they are giving you the first seven words? "You should send me to Hawaii because..." If you take the first seven words they give you, you must then state your reason in 18 words! If you're following the math here, 7 and 18 equals 25.

Helpful Hint # 4 *Find some friends.*

Business Writing is a team sport. Remember, you saw that statement here first.

Every day, you **compete** with thousands of the best letter, memo, proposal, and e-mail writers in the world. That's the "sport" part of the equation. Sports also involves "winning." Winning for you means getting results with your writing. In most sports, the team wins, not an individual.

Yes, I know golf, tennis and other sports feature only one winner.

This helpful hint requires an attitude adjustment for many business people. Let me explain.

If you have an important document to create, ask your friends, co-workers or bosses questions such as the following:

What do you know about this subject?

What do you know about my audience?

What would you be looking for in a piece of writing about this subject?

What do you think my audience would look for in this document?

How To Get It Right When You Write

How should I approach this subject?

I am not suggesting you call one of those interminable meetings. I suggest, rather, you ask others those questions as you walk to lunch or to a file cabinet. If the document is important enough, call three or four of your friends on the phone and spend five minutes to gather some ideas before you start to write. They will help you get your creative juices flowing.

After you have finished your first draft, ask your friends to review that draft before you send it out. The 480 words a minute in your friends' heads are not the same as the 480 words in your head. Your friends are looking at your words for the first time. They will find things in your writing you never dreamed you put in there.

After reading your writing, your friends will likely give you comments such as, "I don't understand this part.," "What do you mean by this?" "You forgot _____," "You can't say that." "You misspelled some words."

Receiving these comments from your friends is a lot better than receiving them from your bosses or your customers.

If you complete a writing task at 9:15 and read it to yourself at 9:16, you are not really reading it. You are **remembering** all the great ideas you wished to express. In many instances, you don't even see the words. This is how "typos," misspellings, incomplete sentences, incorrect grammar, and structure problems occur.

Helpful Hint # 5 *Use a 24-hour drawer.*

This means putting what you have written in your desk drawer for one day before sending it out. Yes, I know, you don't have time for that. I am constantly amazed in American business that we never have time to do it right, but we always find time to do it over.

In the previous chapter, you learned the four stages of writing. Everything we're discussing now falls in the **Prewriting stage**. In the **Writing stage**, we use the creative side of our brain. In the **Editing stage**, we use the analytical side of our brain. Using a 24-hour drawer means allowing enough time for your brain to switch from the creative to the analytical. This takes time.

Fire! Ready! Aim!

I'm not crazy or naive. I realize in most business situations you don't have time for a 24-hour drawer. But, the more time you allow between the writing and editing stages, the better your writing becomes.

I'm sure many of you have read something you wrote six days, six weeks or six months ago and did not recognize it as coming from you. This happens because of the **Speed Traps** we discussed earlier. The thoughts and feelings we have on Monday are not the same as those we have on Tuesday. Our thoughts, feelings, pressures, and even opinions change quickly.

The pressures of today's business world often force us to create a short memo, letter, or e-mail and send it out without enough time to put aside, run through our spell checkers or grammar checkers, or give it to our friends. We all go through it.

Helpful Hint # 6 *Read your writing out loud.*

That is not an invitation to a rubber room. That is a good technique to test your writing. If you read your writing out loud, you will see how long the sentences are. If you read your writing out loud, you may find out that you are running out of breath before you are running out of words. If you run out of breath before you run out of words, you know your sentences are too long. Remember the helpful hint - average 18 words per sentence? That 18 word average will help ensure you don't run out of breath too often.

You should also read your writing to test the rhythm of your sentences. Words do have rhythm. Reading your writing out loud allows you to hear that rhythm. You cannot hear or feel that rhythm if you read your writing in your mind. When you read silently you tend to read for content and often do not even see some of the words.

I am sure many of you have experienced typing the words *the* two times in a row. The chances are pretty high that if you proofread the sentence internally you might miss the error. The reason for that again is that you are reading for the the message and not necessarily looking at all the words. How many of you saw the word *the* repeated in the previous sentence?

Some of you may have experienced a situation like this. You give your writing to a friend to read. Your friend reads your writing and says, "Sounds good to me." Notice what your friend said, **"Sounds** good." That means your friend heard and felt the rhythm of your words. You cannot hear the rhythm of your words by reading it to yourself. The reason is you skip half the words. Reading your writing out loud forces you to slow down to look at each word. Looking at each word helps ensure the sentence says exactly what you want it to mean.

Helpful Hint # 7 *Proofread, proofread, proofread.*

Obviously, **Helpful Hint # 7** stresses the importance of proofreading. I use the word proofread three times because I am reminding you that you don't have to do all that proofreading. Remember, I said find some friends? You should do one version of proofreading. Your friends should do another. Your spell checkers and grammar checkers should do another.

I also stress the importance of proofreading because the minimum you should do it is twice. The first time you proofread, you proofread for content. Is your message clear, correct, concise, complete, and conversational? The second time you proofread, you proofread for mechanics. By mechanics, I mean your spelling, punctuation, grammar, format, and approach.

Remember, this is the proofreading stage. By this time in the writing process, you should have gone through extensive editing. Proofreading is your last shot at getting your writing to the point where you will get the results you're looking for.

Yes, You Can

Participants in my workshops offer me another reason why they have struggled with business writing. This reason relates to a collection of rules of grammar that simply don't exist, shouldn't exist, can be bent, or at least questioned. I call this section **Yes, You Can** because these "rules" trigger an inner voice that says, "Never do this" and "You cannot do that."

Fire! Ready! Aim!

Yes, You Can end a sentence with a preposition.

That is one rule I definitely do not agree with. Please reread that last sentence and check out how I ended the sentence. I ended it with a preposition. If you find a rule in print that tells you ending a sentence with a preposition is poor writing, call me; write me; fax me; e-mail me. I want to know if this rule does exist in any book.

Rule 1080 of the eighth edition of the Gregg Reference Manual states, "Whether or not a sentence should end with a preposition depends on the emphasis and effect desired." It then goes on to give examples of informal, formal, stilted and natural sentences and the impact ending a sentence with a preposition could have.

Rudolph Flesch, in ***The Art of Readable Writing*** refers to a story about Professor C. C. Fries who once told his students that there was no such rule as "Never use a preposition at the end of a sentence." Fries went on to inform his students that he should know about such things because he was the president of the National Council of Teachers of English.

A participant in one of my workshops shouted for joy when he learned he could end a sentence with a preposition. Here's what he told the class. "I wish I had this writing program two days ago. I wasted an hour yesterday trying to rewrite a sentence I wrote that ended with a preposition. If I had known I could end a sentence with a preposition, I would have saved myself an hour."

Yes, a preposition is something you can end a sentence with.

Yes, You Can start a sentence with "because."

Yes, you can start a sentence with the word, "because." Because you bought this book, you will learn to write faster and get better results. That last sentence started with "because," and clearly communicated my guarantee to you.

Warning:

Because many people heeded this dumb rule, they created a vacuum they needed to fill. They could not use "**because**" to start the sentence, so they substituted the word, "**since**." This is incorrect because the word "**since**" implies "time."

> **Since he will be in Boston, he will visit the Boston branch.**

That sentence is incorrect. It should read:

> ***Because he will be in Boston, he will visit the Boston branch.***

The following sentence uses the word "**since**" correctly to denote "time".

> ***Since his accident, he has experienced headaches.***

This sentence lets us know that before his accident, he probably did not experience the headaches. After the **time** of his accident, the headaches started.

Another incorrect substitute for "**because**" is the word "**as.**" That doesn't work either because the word "**as**" pertains to "condition."

> **If you will be deplaning, please place your belongings in the overhead rack as our maintenance crew prepares the cabin for our next flight.**

That sentence is incorrect. It should read:

> ***If you will be deplaning, please place your belongings in the overhead rack because our maintenance crew prepares the cabin for our next flight.***

Using *"as"* in the sentence implies that you should wait for the maintenance crew to come aboard so that you can place your belongings *while* they prepare the cabin.

In that instance, you use *"as"* to imply **time**.

The actual intent of the sentence is to inform you of the **reason** you should place your belongings in the overhead racks. That reason is that the maintenance crew will be preparing the cabin.

The following sentence uses the word "**as**" correctly to denote condition.

> ***As the manger of the department, she became the spokesperson for the group.***

Fire! Ready! Aim!

Let's review those three ideas.

> Use *"because"* to explain a ***reason***.
>
> Use *"since"* to indicate ***time***.
>
> Use *"as"* to denote a ***condition***.

Yes, You Can use one sentence paragraphs.

I find very little logic and no reasonable justification for forcing myself to use two sentences when one will work.

If you can convey an idea clearly, completely and correctly in one sentence, please do so.

Please do not interpret my words to mean that **all** paragraphs should be one sentence long. I suggest you save the one sentence paragraphs for those ideas you want to express powerfully.

For example, I recommend you use a one sentence paragraph to begin an important letter, memo, report, or proposal. This techniques allows you to start with an idea that readers can focus on, read quickly, and remember easily.

I suspect this strange "rule" comes from what we learned about the outlining format. Check out the following:

```
I
    A.
    B.
II
    A.
III
    A.
    B.
    C.
```

Your teachers would quickly point out that you needed at least two letters (A and B) before you could create a Roman Numeral. That means the above outline form would be incorrect because Roman Numeral II had only an A.

From the rules of outlining, some implied that paragraphs had to have more than one sentence. Wrong!! Don't use all one-sentence paragraphs. But, don't force yourself to write two sentences when you can complete your thought in one.

In a following section, you will see an example of how to use one sentence paragraphs.

Yes, You Can use the same word twice in a sentence.

If you send me a copy of a rule that appears anywhere in a popularly accepted grammar book that tells you not to use the same word twice in the same sentence, I will send you $100. Please tell me how I could have written that last sentence without using the word "you" three times.

I'm glad John F. Kennedy ignored that rule. "Ask not what your country can do for you; ask what you can do for your country."

I hope you realize what you can accomplish once you let go of some of the dumb rules you have learned. Be honest with me. Were you offended because I used the word "you" 4 times in the last sentence?

Yes, You Can begin a sentence with "**But**," "**And**," "**Nor**," or "**Or**."

As with one-sentence paragraphs, you can use your literary license occasionally for impact, effect, or mental breaks. The key word becomes "occasionally." As a mental break, these devices perform a useful function. I take my cue on beginning a sentence with *"**But**,"* *"**And**,"* *"**Nor**,"* or *"**Or**"* from a higher power. One of the all time great television newscasters, Walter Cronkite, called the most trusted man in America at the time, ended his newscasts by saying, "And that's the way it is..."

Did the English teachers of the world picket to have him thrown off television? No! Did his colleagues make fun of him? No! They called him the **dean** of American broadcasters.

Yes, you can begin a sentence with *"**But**,"*, *"**And**,"* *"**Nor**,"* or *"**Or**."* I recommend you do not use this technique more than twice a page.

Let me share with you a graphic I created to show my workshop participants the impact of one-sentence paragraphs and using *"**And**"* to begin a sentence.

Fire! Ready! Aim!

> Today's economy has produced more millionaires than in any other time in history.
>
> Word word word word word word word word word word word word word word word word word word word. Word word word word word word word word word word word word word word word word word word.
>
> Word word word word word word word word word word word word word word word word word. Word word word word word word word word word word word word word word word word word word word word word word word. Word word word word word word word word word word word word word word word word word.
>
> And, he made $10,000,000.
>
> Word word word word word word word word word word word word word word word word word. Word word word word word word word word word word word word word word word word word word word word word word word. Word word word word word word word word word word word word word word word word word.

Yes, You Can use contractions.

Yes, you can use contractions in business writing. Should you? I can't tell you that. Whether or not you use them depends on your purpose, your audience, and whatever your company business writing style guide recommends.

I like and use contractions because they carry a natural and conversational tone. I likewise can be convinced I shouldn't use them because half of them denote a negative tone, and the other half derive from weak verbs. I will discuss negative tone and weak verbs later in the book. If you want your letters, memos or reports to convey a personal, conversational tone, use contractions. If your bosses tell you not to use them, drop them (the contractions, not your bosses).

Yes, You Can split infinitives.

Your business writing may call for you to sometimes split infinitives.

An infinitive is a phrase that contains the word "to" followed by a verb. *I want to go home*. In that sentence, "to go" shows up as an infinitive. The more words you place between the word "to" and "go," the longer your brain has to focus on that phrase to understand what it means or how to use it in the sentence.

For example, consider the following sentence. " I want to quickly and without fear of economic or professional loss get out of this situation."

Nine words separate the word "to" from the action you want to perform. That requires your brain to hold those nine words in a buffer until you get to the complete idea. That wastes time and brain power and can confuse or turn off your readers.

Now read the sentence with an "unsplit" infinitive. "I want to get out of this situation quickly and without fear of economic or professional loss." The sentence becomes clear, easy-to-read, easy-to-understand and does not tax your brain.

As I suggested, unless your company style guide tells you not to do so, you can split infinitives by one or two words.

Consider the following sentences:

> *"I want you to quickly run down stairs and get me an adjustable wrench."*
>
> *"I want you to very quickly run down stairs and get me an adjustable wrench."*

The first sentence split the infinitive by one word; the second sentence by two words. I believe all of you understood each of those sentences and would have no problem with them.

Technically speaking, an infinitive does not always have to include the word to. For example, consider the sentence

Fire! Ready! Aim!

We assign new members tasks that help them network with other members.

That sentence implies the word to before the word network. It means, **"...help them to network."**

I recommend that you not split infinitives by more that two words.

Grammar checkers, built into or added to your word processing programs, will find split infinitives for you. You must then decide if you want to or need to change the sentence. These grammar checkers allow you to set the number of words by which you can split an infinitive.

I recommend you set it at **3**. That means anytime your grammar checker finds an infinitive split by **3** or more words, it will stop and ask you what you want to do about it. I recommend setting it at **3** because sometimes you may want to or need to split the infinitive by one, or maybe, even two words.

Did you catch the split infinitive in the first sentence of this section? That sentence read, "Your business writing may call for you to sometimes split infinitives."

Yes, You Can save the Topic Sentence for the last thing you write.

The Topic Sentence normally is the first sentence or the first two sentences of a letter or a paragraph. Although the Topic Sentence appears first, no rule in any language says you must write it first. Many people waste too much time trying to create the perfect Topic Sentence before they continue on with their message.

If you are one of these people who stare at a blank sheet of paper or a computer screen looking for that perfect sentence, move on. Start writing the body of your document. After you have completed that task, the Topic Sentence will become easier to write. This technique will probably save you a lot of time and improve the quality of your Topic Sentence.

Yes, You Can begin a sentence with "I".

When I reveal this piece of wisdom to seminar participants, I pause and listen to their reactions. Most seminar participants tell me this is one rule that was pounded into their heads. I have a real problem with that. Participants tell me this rule comes from their English teachers who said, "Never start a sentence with 'I' because it sounds like you're bragging." That's dumb. Yes, you can start a sentence with "I."

I know my participants are not lying to me because I had a similar situation happen to me when I was writing my Masters Thesis. I started a sentence with "I" and the professor, who was my advisor, told me I couldn't do that.

I said, "Alan, why not?" To which I heard total silence. Again I asked, "Alan, why not?" And, the answer I got was, "Because we don't do that in academia." And again I asked, "Why not?"

At this point I realized I was squeezing too hard and backed off. I'm no fool. He was my audience, and I wanted my Masters degree.

So, I asked him, "Alan, how should I start that sentence?" He gave me a nine word phrase, followed by a comma, to use to begin my sentence. So, I used it.

Let me share the sentence with you and you decide whether or not I needed those nine words and the comma in the sentence.

> *To give an example which the author has used, I often begin a program by having the participants stand and introduce themselves.*

Get Real!

Yes, You Can use "I" in business letters.

You can and should use the personal pronouns "I," "you," "we," "he," "she" in business letters.

No matter what job or industry you're in, you are in a people-to-people business. Many companies and governmental agencies seem to have forgotten that. If you are to succeed in business writing, you must learn how to use the pronouns "I" and "you" effectively. Let me give you an example of how this works.

Pretend that I sell widgets. You ordered 18 purple widgets from me. What you received were 13 pink widgets. You now have the wrong quantity and the wrong color. So, you send me a "nastygram" telling me of your dissatisfaction with getting 13 pink widgets rather than the 18 purple widgets you ordered.

I send you a reply that reads as follows:

> We received your claim that you received 13 pink widgets. We checked the warehouse, and we do have purple widgets in stock. We are prepared to ship you 18 purple widgets as soon as possible.
>
> Your comments are greatly appreciated.

Or, you receive this letter.

> Thank you for bringing our error to my attention.
>
> I called the warehouse and found out that we do have purple widgets in stock. I will ship you 18 purple widgets on June 1. If you do not receive them by June 3, please call me at extension 2929.

Which letter would you rather receive? Most people in my seminars tell me they would rather receive the second letter. The reasons for this are simple. The second letter is more personal, and shows accountability and responsibility. Also, the second letter shows that the company cares about the reader as an individual, not as a number in the computer. The reader received a personal letter rather than a form letter.

Think about what's going on in the company that wrote the first letter. They stated, "We checked the warehouse." That must be a strangely managed company if every employee must assemble in the warehouse to check on product availability for each customer problem. That's what the sentence implies by using the word "we."

Don't be afraid to use the personal pronoun "I" in business letters. I highly recommend you do so.

So, how do you know when to use "I" and when not to. The following examples should help you.

> Do I recommend you use "I" all the time? No! In most business writing, I promote the idea of focusing on the reader. I will show you how to do this as we go through the different sections of this book. For now, I think a few examples will allow me to explain this concept.

The text in the above text box used the pronoun "I" as the subject of each sentence. Check out how much more reader-focused it becomes when the reader becomes the subject.

> Should you use "I" all the time. No! In most business writing, you should focus on the reader. You will learn how to do this as we journey though the different sections of this book. For now, remember that reader-focus is more important than "I" focus.

But, don't be afraid to use "I" when doing so makes sense. For example, consider the two following sentences.

It has recently come to my attention that you were selected to receive the Medal of Honor.

versus

I just learned that you were selected to receive the Medal of Honor.

No contest. Definitely use the second sentence rather than the first.

Fire! Ready! Aim!

Subject - Verb - Relationship

If you gain anything from this book, I hope you remember two things. The first is that for your writing to get results, you must understand and focus on your **purpose** and your **audience**.

The second important lesson very simply states:

The key to good writing is the Subject - Verb - Relationship. That's it! Forget the fluffy adverbs. Forget the flowery adjectives. **The key to good writing is the Subject - Verb - Relationship.**

Here's what that means. In business writing, what do people want to know? They want to know **Who** is doing what. **What** is doing what? **How** does it happen? **Why** does it happen? **Where** does it happen? **When** does it happen? **To whom** does it happen? You express this information by using the **Subject - Verb - Relationship.**

Figure 1 graphically displays the relevance of this concept.

Figure 1

Subject	Verb	Relationship
Who or What	Is Doing	What

To explain the concept of the **Subject - Verb - Relationship**, let's review a sentence.

Our high school basketball team won the state championship.

In that sentence, *high school basketball team* becomes the **subject.** Yes, I know your English teachers would say *team* is the **subject** and *high school* and *basketball* are adjectives modifying team. I use *high school basketball team* as a unit. If I have a fire at my house, I want to see fire trucks, not dump trucks arrive to help me. Anyway, *high school basketball team* becomes the **subject.**

Won becomes the **verb** in the sentence. Remember that a **verb** is a word that shows action. Action helps you see the motion or activity taking place.

State championship becomes the **relationship**. That relationship completes the picture the writer wants to paint for you. Simply saying "Our high school basketball team won" does not give you a complete picture. You need that **relationship** to show the importance of the *winning*.

Let's try another graphic example.

>   *A dog bit the man.*

In that sentence, *dog* becomes the **subject**, *bit* becomes the **verb** and *man* shows or completes the **relationship**.

I believe all of you created some mental picture, feeling or attitude as you read the sentence, *A dog bit the man.*

Let's see if the picture, feeling or attitude changes if we change the **Subject - Verb - Relationship** using the same words.

>   *The man bit the dog.*

I hope you got a different picture with that sentence. The words stayed the same; the **Subject - Verb - Relationship** changed. *Man* became the subject, *bit* remains as the verb, but *dog* now shows the relationship.

People think and relate in terms of pictures. People think and relate in terms of motion. Consider the word, *Hawaii*. When you read the word, *Hawaii*, what kind of mental pictures came to you? You did not merely focus on the word. Your mind started creating pictures.

If I said, *A man walked down the street*, you might get one picture. But, if I said, *Abraham Lincoln staggered down Pennsylvania Avenue*, you would get a different, and perhaps more graphic or specific picture.

Headline writers know the value of the **Subject - Verb - Relationship**. Consider the following headlines and the pictures and emotions they create.

>   **Man walks on moon.**
>
>   **Local man wins state lottery.**
>
>   **Blizzard hits Northeast.**

Fire! Ready! Aim!

I hope you can keep a mental picture of **Figure 1** in your minds as we work our way through the next couple of chapters.

Most good business writing falls apart in the middle of **Figure 1**. This happens when writers do not use **verbs** correctly. In fact, not only do they use **verbs** incorrectly, they sometimes destroy perfectly *good verbs*.

As we progress through this book, I will share with you at least five different ways writers destroy good verbs. Every time you destroy a good verb, you cloud the picture of who or what is performing the action. That means the subject of the sentence becomes unclear. If the reader does not understand clearly who or what is doing what, the reader becomes unsure. Even worse, the reader may **assume** information that you do not intend as your message.

CHAPTER REVIEW

The following points highlight the more important topics discussed in this chapter. Scan them to see how many you can explain to someone else. If you cannot, I hope you invest the time to review them before moving on to the next section.

Five Things You Must Know Before You Write

1. *Your business writing is a valuable corporate asset.*

    People decide important business issues based on what you write.

2. *The biggest time waster in business writing is spending too much time in the Writing Stage.*

3. *You can eliminate your fear and dread of writing by knowing its source.*

    Big People Like Big Words - Big People Like Big Sentences.

    100 Words - 10 Pages - 2 Blue Books

4. *To become a better writer, you must understand the communication process.*

5. *Speed Traps can slow you down.*

    The Speed Traps are: Think Speed - See Speed - Read Speed - Speak Speed - Write Speed

Seven Helpful Hints

Helpful Hint # 1   Write to be understood, not to overwhelm.

Helpful Hint # 2   Become intimate with your grammar checkers.

Helpful Hint # 3   Average 18 words per sentence.

Fire! Ready! Aim!

Helpful Hint # 4	**Find some friends.**
	Business writing is a team sport.
Helpful Hint # 5	**Use a 24-hour drawer.**
Helpful Hint # 6	**Read your writing out loud.**
Helpful Hint # 7	**Proofread, proofread, proofread.**

Yes, You Can

- **End a sentence with a preposition**
- **Start a sentence with "because"**
- **Use one-sentence paragraphs**
- **Use the same word twice in a sentence**
- **Begin a sentence with "But," "And," "Nor," or "Or"**
- **Use contractions**
- **Split infinitives**
- **Save the topic sentence for the last thing you write**
- **Begin a sentence with "I"**
- **Use "I" in business letters**

Subject - Verb - Relationship

Subject	Verb	Relationship
Who or What	Is Doing	What

"Your business writing is a valuable corporate asset."

Chapter Three
Mommy and Daddy Need To Party

This chapter expands on three concepts you read about earlier in the book.

First, many people waste too much time with their writing. You will learn how to save time.

Second, you learned that many people remember only a numerical need to get to **100 Words - 10 Pages and 2 Blue Books**. Helpful Hint #3 suggests you *average 18 words per sentence*. In this chapter, you will recognize how you constructed sentences averaging 20 to 24 words. And, you will learn how to quickly, easily, and painlessly get back to an 18 word average.

Third, you will learn the five ways people destroy good writing by using verbs incorrectly. This chapter deals exclusively with those five ways. The next chapter reviews other common errors in writing.

To help you recognize and remember these errors, the heading will contain the word **Avoid**.

Let's get started.

Avoid Weak Verbs

Weak Verbs fall into three categories.

The first category centers around what English teachers call State of Being Verbs or Linking Verbs. The verbs include:

Am   Are   Is   Was   Were   Be   Been

In his book, *Talking Straight*, Lee Iacocca offers his "little commandments of management." He sums up his third commandment, by telling us to "Write the way you talk. If you don't talk that way, don't write that way."

Consider the sentence:

I am in receipt of your check.

How many of you ever called someone on the phone, waited for an answer, and as soon as the person answered, you said, *"I am in receipt of your check."*

Do you talk that way? I don't think so. At least I hope you don't. Then, as Mr. Iacocca says, "don't write that way." I hope all of you would say, *"I received your check."*

In the helpful hints discussion, I suggested that you should keep your writing conversational. That's what I meant by that. In conversation, you would not say to someone, "I am in receipt of your check." You would say, "I received your check."

The original sentence, "I am in receipt of your check," contained seven words. The conversational version contains four.

Why would normally rational, reasonable people, pressured by time in their jobs, want to write seven words when they could save themselves and their readers time by writing only four? You know the answer - **100 Words - 10 Pages - 2 Blue Books**. Automatically, when people write, they feel the ever present academic ghosts haunting their minds.

The original sentence used *am* as the verb. That **Weak Verb** forced the writer to use more words and to use an unnatural, sometimes confusing style to express a very simple thought.

The reason for the length and structure of that sentence now becomes clear. We all felt the artificial need to reach our goals of **100 Words - 10 Pages - 2 Blue Books**.

Now let's explore *how* we accomplished the task.

To understand *how* we got to **100 Words - 10 Pages - 2 Blue Books**, we must first recall and clearly understand two ideas we discussed in **Chapter Two**. The first concept is the **Subject - Verb - Relationship**. The second is my suggestion about using your grammar checkers.

As we explore the five ways writers misuse verbs, we will see how critical the concept of the **Subject - Verb - Relationship** becomes. Before we do that, let me explain *how* and *why* grammar checkers relate to our discussion of **Weak Verbs**.

Mommy and Daddy Need To Party

Many word processing packages contain grammar checkers as part of the standard software. Some people bought them as stand alone products hoping they would cure all their writing ills. Most of my workshop attendees tell me they try these grammar checkers and become frustrated or confused. They complain these products take more time and add more trouble than they're worth.

I understand this frustration. Yet, these products can prove to be unbelievably valuable to you.

The main source of frustration falls on the comments and suggestions these grammar checkers flash on the screen. For example, the grammar checkers would read your document and flash a message that you're using too many prepositional phrases. Hang in there with me.

I will show you what these messages mean and more importantly, I will show you how to use them to save time and improve your writing. Both increase your chances of getting better results.

To explain **why** prepositional phrases are important to you, I ask you to again recall the **Subject - Verb - Relationship**. Also, I ask you to mentally return to your seventh grade English teacher telling you that the *subject* of a sentence is always a noun or pronoun. That teacher also told you that a preposition always required an object and that objects of prepositions were always nouns or pronouns.

Here's **why** that's important. Subjects, direct objects, indirect objects and objects of prepositions all require nouns or pronouns. This means the more nouns and pronouns you throw into the sentence, the more you confuse your readers. You force them to play multiple choice mind games to figure out which noun serves as the subject.

This means every time they read one of your sentences, they must unconsciously diagram the sentence in their heads. You hated diagramming sentences when you were a kid! Don't force your readers to go through that agony to try to understand your writing.

For the purpose of this discussion, let's forget direct objects and indirect objects. You will understand why as we progress through the book. We will focus on **how** objects of prepositions confuse your readers.

Prepositional phrases weaken your writing because they hide the real subject of the sentence – the doer of the action. Hiding the doer of the action clouds the picture and limits your ability to communicate effectively on paper.

I'm sure all of you are familiar with the fact that what people think and what they say can be two different things. Similarly, what people think and what they *write* become two different things.

All of you have experienced this at some point. You clearly understand in your mind what you want to say, but the words you write don't come close to what you mean. Many times, this happens because you use too many prepositional phrases to try to convey on paper an idea you see clearly in your mind.

Now, let's return to our sample sentence.

I am in receipt of your check.

In that sentence, the verb becomes *am*. *Am* is a **Weak Verb**. In that sentence, you will find two prepositional phrases, *in receipt* and *of your check*.

 **YOU NEED A PEN OR PENCIL NOW!**

I am in receipt of your check.

With your pen or pencil, cross out the **Weak Verb** *am* in the sample sentence above. Now cross out the prepositions *in* and *of*. Now cross out the word *receipt* and above it write the word *received*. The sentence now reads:

I received your check.

Instead of seven words, this sentence requires only four to clearly say what you mean. The verb in the sentence becomes the strong verb, *received*. Why would a normally rational, reasonable person use seven words rather than four? **100 Words - 10 Pages - 2 Blue Books**. Now you have seen **why** and **how** people get up to **100 Words - 10 Pages - 2 Blue Books**. You now also understand how quickly, easily and painlessly you can take your writing from 20 to 24 words down to your target of 18 words sentence.

Check this out.

> **I am of the opinion we should stop the project.**

Get real! What does this really mean?

> ***I think we should stop the project.***

In the revised version, we:

- Shortened the sentence from ten words to seven
- Wiped out the Weak Verb, ***am***
- Inserted a strong verb, ***think***
- Eliminated a prepositional phrase
- Wrote in a more conversational manner

Let's try another example.

 **YOU NEED A PEN OR PENCIL NOW!**

> **They are in need of more control in their lives.**

In the above sample sentence, you find three prepositional phrases.

> **in need**   **of more control**   **in their lives**

For the moment, we will concentrate on just the first two. First, cross out the **Weak Verb** *are*. Now cross out the prepositions, *in* and *of*.

The sentence now reads:

They need more control in their lives.

You eliminated three words from the sentence. The words you eliminated offered absolutely, positively no more power, no meaning, no benefit. Why would normally rational, reasonable people use 10 words rather than seven? **100 Words - 10 Pages - 2 Blue Books. Big People Like Big Words - Big People Like Big Sentences**.

Above, you found three prepositional phrases in the original example. You then eliminated the first two. Now lets work on the third one. Let's use our revised sentence:

 **YOU NEED A PEN OR PENCIL NOW!**

They need more control in their lives.

In that sentence, cross out the preposition *in*. To do that, you need to cross out the pronoun *they*. Move *their lives* to the beginning to become the subject. The sentence now reads:

Their lives need more control.

Notice that the first two times you changed the sentences, you replaced the verb. In this revision, you changed the subject.

Remember, the key to good writing - **Subject - Verb - Relationship**. That's where you find the meaning. That's where you find the power.

Some of you might think, "Wait a minute, Al. You just changed the meaning of that sentence." Thank you for noticing. Indeed, for some of you, I may have changed the meaning of the sentence. If you noticed a change in meaning, great! If you didn't notice a change, great! Either way, you win. You've begun to understand that the way you arrange the words in the sentence, can impact the meaning and therefore the results you get. You have total control of the **Subject - Verb - Relationship**.

If you like the sentence, *Their lives need more control*, understand how the meaning and impact came about. In the original version of the sentence, ***their lives*** served as the object of the preposition ***in***.

In the revised version, you elevated the importance of those words from a secondary position – object of preposition – to primary importance, the **subject** of the sentence.

Remember that concept. As you travel through this book, you will see many examples from typical business writing where the authors buried the real subjects of their sentences as objects of prepositions. When this happens, this forces the sentences to become longer. Longer is not better. Longer is the devise created to attain **100 Words - 10 pages - 2 Blue Books. Big People Like Big Words - Big People Like Big Sentences**.

Let's try another.

 **YOU NEED A PEN OR PENCIL NOW!**

We are in agreement with your assertions.

In the above sentence, you find two prepositional phrases:

    in agreement   **with your assertions**

Again with your pen or pencil, cross out the **Weak Verb** *are*. For the moment, we will deal with only the first prepositional phrase, *in agreement*. So, cross out the preposition, ***in***. Now, draw a line through the letters ***m,e,n,*** and ***t***. The sentence now reads:

We agree with your assertions.

You have now wiped out 10 typing spaces from the original sentence.

One of the objectives I hope you checked as a reason for reading this book was to make your business writing more personal. Let me show you how to accomplish that.

Let me ask you a question. Do you agree with ***assertions***, or do you agree with ***people***? I hope you said ***people***.

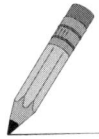 **YOU NEED A PEN OR PENCIL NOW!**

In the revised example sentence, cross out the *r* in *your* and cross out the word, *assertions*. The sentence now reads:

We agree with you.

Notice how the sentence became **shorter**, and it became **more personal**. You are now talking *to* your audience, not *at* them.

Technically, all you need to write is: **We agree.** *We* becomes the subject; *agree* becomes the verb. The key to good writing is the **Subject - Verb - Relationship**.

Do I suggest you write all sentences this simply? No! Remember the helpful hint, **"average 18 words a sentence?"** That's why you don't write all two or five or 10 word sentences. Notice, however, the impact a two or three word sentence brings to a paragraph. Short sentences work.

Let me show you two more very common examples of **Weak Verbs** wasting typing spaces and impact.

I am suggesting we change the procedure.

If you eliminate the **Weak Verb** and the *ing*, you shorten the sentence and get greater impact with:

I suggest we change the procedure.

Here's another popular business sentence.

This letter is to confirm the special offer I made to you last week.

Drop the *is to* and add an *s* to *confirm* and the sentence reads:

This letter confirms the special offer I made to you last week.

The second category of **Weak Verbs** include what English teachers call helping verbs or auxiliary verbs. These verbs include:

Have	**Has**	**Had**
Do	**Did**	**Done**

The above list become helping verbs when they help a main verb express the tense of the verb. For example, consider the following two sentences.

I ran a mile in five minutes today.

I have run a mile in five minutes many times.

The first example talks about an action performed once. The second refers to actions performed a number of times in the past. This is a logical, practical use of these verbs.

However, we sometimes use these verbs to weaken our writing. Consider the following sample sentence.

I have instructions to award you a bonus.

In that sentence, "have" stands alone as the main verb. You may feel this sentence says everything you need to say. However, let's look deeper into the reasons behind the sentence or the "real" meaning of it.

Indeed, the sentence states a fact. Notice how the tone and the message change while the length stays the same in the following:

I received instructions to award you a bonus.

Our CEO asked me to award you a bonus.

Congratulations! Your hard work earned you a bonus.

Congratulations! You will receive a bonus for your hard work.

These four sentences help explain two major concepts of this book. First, they show the importance of selecting the correct verb to convey your meaning. The original sentence sounded like you awarded the bonus only because you were ordered to do so. Or, the reader might have picked up a hint that you felt the person did not deserve it. The reader might also have sensed a little jealousy in the sentence.

If someone said to me or wrote to me using the original sentence my reaction would have been, "Who gave you those instructions?"

Second, those four examples clearly explain the value of the **Subject - Verb - Relationship** model. We started with the thought, "I have instructions to award you a bonus." From this, we can use *I*, *CEO*, *Your hard work*, or *you* as the subject of the new and improved sentence.

The new **Strong Verbs** become *received*, *asked*, *earned*, and *will receive*.

Look how the relationships change – *instruction*, *me*, *you*, *bonus*.

Let's try another example.

I had an enjoyable time at the party.

My wife told me the sentence sounded like "lip service." The sentence comes across as cold and insincere. It also sounds like an obligation. You can shorten the sentence and improve its tone by using a strong verb.

I enjoyed your party.

The third category of **Weak Verbs** hints of action but really doesn't clearly define the action. They also force you to use more words. These verbs include:

        Make   **Take**   **Give**

For example, let's use a sentence we see often in business.

Our manager made a recommendation that we sell the used goods at half price.

The manager did not *make* anything. The manager *recommended*. Give people credit for what they do. The sentence should read:

Our manager recommended we sell the used goods at half price.

Notice in the last sentence that I also eliminated the word *that*.

Bonus Idea

In **Chapter Two**, one of the helpful hints said, "Read your writing out loud." To decide whether or not you need the word *that* in the sentence, read the sentence out loud two times.

The first time you read it, leave the word *that* in the sentence. The second time, leave it out.

The sentence above reads:

Notice in the last sentence that I also eliminated the word *that*.

Read it out loud. Go on, read it out loud. No one is watching.

Okay. Now read it without the two **thats**.

Notice in the last sentence I also eliminated the word.

See, it works.

Reading the sentence out loud showed you that you could drop the first *that*, but you needed the second one.

Let's try one more using *made*.

Ian made a point that the club treasury was painfully low.

Ian did not "make" anything. He ***pointed out***, ***mentioned***, ***stressed*** or ***warned***.

Ian warned that the club treasury was painfully low.

Let's try a sentence using *take*.

The committee will take a look at your ideas.

Again, the committee will not *take* anything.

The committee will look at your ideas.

The committee will review your ideas.

Before we leave the discussion of the third category, let me offer an example of using *give*.

Please give some thought to becoming a sponsor.

Rather than using **give** as the **Weak Verb** and *thought* as a noun, let's change the sentence to say what we really mean.

Please think about becoming a sponsor.

Let me share with you another personal example that illustrates the point about the power of **Strong Verbs.**

My oldest daughter blessed our family with twins. A month before the twin's second birthday, Christine asked me to help her create party invitations on my computer. I told her to create the text of the message, and I would show her how to graphically present that on paper. The first two lines of her text read:

Derek and Alexandra are two.

Mommy and Daddy need to have a party.

Grampy suggested the invitation read:

Mommy and Daddy need to party.

This subtle change conveyed what Christine really thought and felt. When my wife, Marylou, proofread the book, she said the original sentence again sounded obligatory. She said it sounded as though Chris did not want to have a party but because she was a mother, she felt forced to have a party. That's not what Chris intended. So we changed the invitation.

Notice that Grampy's version used two less words and changed the noun *party* into a strong verb. Hey, when you're the mother and father of twins, you need to party every once in a while!

Strong verbs and their relationship to the subject create vivid pictures and vivid emotions.

Checking the **Subject - Verb - Relationship** in newspaper headlines normally helps you tell good newspapers from poor ones. For example, consider the following headline.

Contract Rejected At Local High School

Notice how weak that headline is. Who rejected the contract - the school board, the teachers, the tax payers, the state arbitrators, the courts?

Mommy and Daddy Need To Party

Sports writers would vanish without strong verbs.

Pirates Pound Padres

Steelers Dump Dallas

Penguins Win Stanley Cup

I know. You're upset. I'm pushing Pittsburgh. Call me; write me; fax me; e-mail me.

I'm not telling you to eliminate **Weak Verbs** all the time. I'm asking you to look for them in your writing as opportunities to become clear, concise and graphic.

To be fair, let me share a couple of instances where you might want to use **Weak Verbs**.

Calvin was able to influence the outcome.

In my seminars, participants normally do one of two things with that sample sentence. The easiest way to change this sentence to eliminate the **Weak Verb** would be:

Calvin influenced the outcome.

Changing this sentence this way eliminates three words and uses a strong verb that creates a more powerful picture of what Sam did.

Some might have done nothing with this sentence. That also would be legitimate. I am trying to influence you to look for **Weak Verbs** and eliminate them to bring action and power to your sentences.

However, you will never be able to eliminate **Weak Verbs** all the time. The verbs that I listed as **Weak Verbs** are more commonly known as **state of being verbs** or **linking verbs.**

State of being verbs show existence or equality. For example, consider the following example:

My name is Al Borowski.

In that sentence, I used *is,* a **state of being** or a **linking verb**, as the main verb. Notice that *name* and *Al Borowski* mean the same thing.

I could also use the example:

The price is $1,000.

In that sentence, ***price*** and ***$1,000*** mean the same thing. In the first example we used **"I am in receipt of your check."** The word "**am**" does not indicate that ***I*** and ***in receipt*** mean the same thing.

In the example above, ***Calvin*** and ***able*** refer to the same person. You can use an adjective after a linking verb to describe or emphasize a characteristic of the person or thing you use as the subject of the sentence.

You can logically use state of being verbs or linking verbs to express an idea like:

Calvin was able to influence the outcome. But, he did not.

Notice the message these two short sentences conveyed. Notice also, I started the second sentence with the word ***but***. Remember in a previous chapter, I suggested that you can use ***but*** or ***and*** to begin a sentence.

Notice the dramatic effect and power the sentence now has even though you use two short sentences, both of which used **Weak Verbs**.

My message and my purpose here is to raise your level of awareness of **Weak Verbs**. I recommend you look for them in your writing or let your computer look for them. Finding them highlights areas where you might improve the power and meaning of your sentences.

Mommy and Daddy Need To Party

Practice Changing Weak Verbs to Strong Verbs

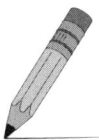 **YOU NEED A PEN OR PENCIL NOW!**

Change the following sentences to eliminate the **Weak Verbs**, become more graphic and specific, stick to the point, and use less words. Remember, you might need to change some subjects as well as the **Weak Verbs** to convey a more powerful message or allow the sentence to read better. After you complete this activity, compare your approach to the alternatives or suggestions I offer. Enjoy.

1. He is desirous of a better station in life.

2. A galootin pin is a contraption that is utilized for the purpose of having a person determine the length of a widget.

3. All new employees will be in attendance at the morning session only.

4. I am of the opinion that we should stop production.

5. Please give some thought to becoming a program chair.

6. We will be sending you further information in early July.

7. They have an offer of a free rental car for every hotel stay in July.

8. We are looking forward to meeting you.

9. The committee will take a look at your situation.

10. You can then make a request to receive an extension on your loan.

Let's Compare Notes

Before comparing notes, let's review a few concepts we have already discussed that affect your writing.

1. You must consider your audience and your purpose.
2. Good writing is clear and concise.
3. Business writing should sound conversational.

If you focus on these points, your sentences will become shorter.

As we compare notes, remember that we are all different. Thus, the way you might change a sentence versus the way I approach it could differ dramatically. This means we are not limited to one "right way." Also, please recognize that most of the sentences you worked on stood alone. You did not enjoy the benefit of knowing the context or the circumstances of the sentences. Thus, the way you interpreted the situation and changed the sentences probably differs from the way others might change them. Let's get started.

Practice Sentence # 1

I am of the opinion that we should stop production.

This is a typical sentence that shows how we got to **100 Words - 10 Pages - 2 Blue Books**.

That sentence simply means:

I think we should stop production.

or

I believe we should stop production.

or

I feel we should stop production.

Practice Sentence # 2

He is desirous of a better station in life.

In this sentence, you might have eliminated the **Weak Verb** *is* and changed the adjective *'desirous'* to the strong verb *desires*. Your sentence would now read,

He desires a better station in life.

or

He desires a better life.

or

He wants a better job.

or

He wants to make more money.

or

He's looking for a new job.

or

He needs a job change.

You may have written something entirely different based on your style, your audience and your purpose. The purpose of this activity is to avoid **Weak Verbs, use fewer words** and to convey a clearer message. The original sentence with the **Weak Verb** contained nine words. The revised samples above used a maximum of seven.

Practice Sentence # 3

A galootin pin is a contraption that is utilized for the purpose of having a person determine the length of a widget.

This sentence becomes weak with the use of the verb *is*. You might have changed this sentence by crossing out the words *is a contraption that is utilized for the purpose of having a person*. You would also have to change the verb *determine* to *determines*.

The sentence would then read:

A galootin pin determines the length of a widget.

You could also shorten and improve this sentence by changing the word *determines* to *measures*. Doing so, you use a two syllable word to replace a three syllable word.

The sentence becomes:

A galootin pin measures the length of a widget.

You could further shorten the sentence by eliminating the word *the* and a preposition to say:

A galootin pin measures a widget's length.

I hope one of your objectives for practicing these editing techniques is to "become more personal with your business writing." Perhaps in the original sentence:

A galootin pin is a contraption that is utilized for the purpose of having a person determine the length of a widget.

the writer did want to become "personal." Did you notice the word, "person" in that sentence?

To accomplish this, you could write:

A galootin pin helps people measure the length of a widget.

or

A galootin pin helps people measure a widget's length.

Practice Sentence # 4

All new employees will be in attendance at the morning session only.

You can shorten this sentence by focusing on the **Weak Verb** *be*. If you eliminate *be*, the sentence reads:

All new employees will attend the morning sessions only.

The verb *be* shows existence. The new employees will not *be* anything; they will *do* something. They will *attend*. Changing the sentence also wipes out three words and four extra letters.

Practice Sentence # 5

Please give some thought to becoming a program chair.

To eliminate the **Weak Verb** in this sentence, you could have written:

Please think about becoming a program chair.

or

Please consider chairing the program.

Practice Sentence # 6

We will be sending you further information in early July.

The easiest way to change this sentence to say the same thing and use less words is to eliminate the **Weak Verb,** *"be"* and the *"ing"* from the word *"sending."*

We will send you further information in early July.

Both the original practice sentence and my suggested revision say the same thing. Some of you might wonder why go through the hassle of changing it. Changing that sentence eliminated six key strokes. If you were to eliminate six key strokes in most of the sentences in your business writing, you could easily turn a two-page letter into one page document.

I am sure most of you would prefer to read a one-page document rather than a two-page document. Your readers are the same. If you send them one-page rather than two-pages, your chances of them reading it and acting upon it increase dramatically.

Practice Sentence # 7

They have an offer of a free rental car with every hotel stay in July.

This sentence uses three less words when you change it to

They offer a free rental car with every hotel stay in July.

Practice Sentence # 8

We are looking forward to meeting you.

Again, eliminating the **Weak Verb**, *are* and *ing* shortens the sentence and says exactly what you mean.

We look forward to meeting you.

Practice Sentence # 9

The committee will take a look at your situation.

Practice sentence number nine contains the **Weak Verb,** *take*. Technically speaking, this sentence is a lie. The committee will not *take* anything.

The committee will look at your situation.

or

The committee will review your situation.

You might also approach this situation from a completely different angle. Rather than sounding autocratic and pompous, you might use this sentence to reveal a more human or customer satisfaction attitude.

This would require you to focus on the person's *situation*, rather than the *committee*. In that original sentence, *committee* is the subject and *situation* is the relationship. You could reverse that approach to say:

Your situation will receive the committee's complete attention.

Changing the sentence and the attitude in this way required a longer sentence. Sometimes you sacrifice your conciseness for the sake of clarity. In this instance, you sacrifice conciseness for customer satisfaction.

Practice Sentence # 10

You can then make a request to receive an extension on your loan.

The above sentence contains thirteen words. You can save time for you and the reader by writing:

You can then request to receive an extension on your loan.

or

You can then request an extension on your loan.

or

You can then request a loan extension.

If **Practice Sentence # 10** relates to **Practice Sentence # 9**, you might need the word *then* in Sentence # 10. If the sentences were not related, you might not need *then.*

Avoid Passive Voice

I believe the biggest problem in business writing today is the overuse of the **Passive Voice**.

The reason for this harkens back to the old academic ghosts, **100 Words - 10 Pages - 2 Blue Books. Big People Like Big Words - Big People Like Big Sentences**. Achieving these goals became easier once you mastered the practice of taking a simple idea and making it cloudier and longer by writing the sentence in the **Passive Voice**.

Those of you with technical writing training can attest to the fact that teachers insisted you write in the **Passive Voice**. "It doesn't matter who did the project. What matters is what was done." Now that you are out of the academic, clinical environment and in the real world of business, you will find most audiences want clear and concise writing. They demand to know who or what is doing what. That means limiting the times you use the **Passive Voice**.

Some of you may have experimented with grammar checkers. You probably found that your grammar checker stopped most often to inform you that you were using the **Passive Voice**. Most of my participants answer the same way when I ask them what they do when their grammar checkers stop for the **Passive Voice**. "I hit *Ignore* and move on."

Let me explain the differences between the **Active** and **Passive Voice**, what they mean to your writing, and how to use the information to make your writing clear and concise.

We will use the following sentences to illustrate the point.

>**Jake sipped the beer.**

In the above example, the verb becomes *sipped*. *Sipped* is a good, strong verb. *Jake* becomes the subject of the sentence. Jake also is the person who performed the action of the verb *sipped*.

How To Get It Right When You Write

> "When the subject of your sentence performs the action described in the verb, your sentence displays the active voice."

Let's compare that to the **Passive Voice**. For that, we will use the example:

The beer was sipped by Jake.

In that sentence, the verb becomes *was sipped*. *Was* is a **Weak Verb**. Now you have a **Weak Verb** helping a strong verb. Does that make any sense to you? That's like having a rock teach you how to fly. The subject of the sentence becomes *beer*. The beer is **not** performing the action of *sipping*. Who sipped the beer? *Jake*. Do you see what happened to *Jake*? He showed up way at the end of the sentence as an object of a preposition. How embarrassing - an object of a preposition! If *Jake* were important, where would he be? Up front, as the subject of the sentence. What is the key to good writing? The **Subject - Verb - Relationship!**

The first example in the **Active Voice** uses four words. The example in the **Passive Voice** used seven words. Why would normally rational, reasonable people, pressured by time in their jobs, want to write seven words when they could write four? You know the answer—**100 Words - 10 Pages - 2 Blue Books. Big People Like Big Words - Big People Like Big Sentences**. Automatically, when people write, they feel the ever present academic ghosts haunting their minds.

Let's try another example.

The money was donated by a wealthy patron.

In that example, the verb becomes *was donated*. The subject of the sentence is *money*. Who donated the money? The *wealthy patron*. Where do you find the *wealthy patron*? At the end of the sentence as the object of the preposition *by*.

You can turn that sentence into the active voice by saying:

A wealthy patron donated the money.

Doing so, you eliminated the words *was* and *by.* You used less words and put the emphasis on the person who donated the money.

Okay, the skeptics want *money* to remain as the subject.

The money came from a wealthy donor.

Let's look at the **Passive Voice** from another angle.

The students were sent a copy of the exam.

This sentence shows an example of the **Passive Voice** where the doer of the action is not mentioned. Thus, to change the sentence back into the active voice, you need to supply the doer of the action as the subject.

You might say:

The teacher sent the students a copy of the exam.

In this revision, you added one word to the sentence but painted a much more precise and graphic picture. On the other hand, you might want to keep *students* as the subject of the sentence. To accomplish this, you would change the verb to reflect the proper action.

The students received a copy of the exam.

In review, you find the **Passive Voice** in several ways. **Passive Voice** means:

- you find a **Weak Verb** helping a strong verb.
- the subject of the sentence is not performing the action of the verb.
- the person or thing performing the action shows up at the end of the sentence as an object of the preposition. Sometimes, the person or thing performing the action never shows up.

The **Passive Voice** can weaken your writing in another way. Consider the message of the following sentence:

I have been given instructions to award you a bonus.

At first glance, this might seem like completely good news. But, consider the tone of this message. The person receiving the message will receive a bonus. That's good news. The question now becomes, who had given the instructions? This sentence sounds like the writer really did not want to give the reader the bonus, but someone forced, required or demanded the writer to do so.

To change this sentence to the active voice may actually require more words. But, look at the dramatic, positive impact the message sends.

> ***Mr. Scott, our president, asked me to award you this bonus.***

You can, of course, shorten it to:

> ***Mr. Scott asked me to award you this bonus.***

Sometimes writers use compound verbs in the **Passive Voice** and really confuse their readers. Consider the following sentence.

> **The new software will be installed by the first of the month and will be used for all new employee applications.**

Notice the compound verb, ***will be installed*** and ***will be used***. The confusion comes about when you try to determine who will do the installing and who will do the using. Will they be the same people or the same departments? Will one department install the software and another use it? This sentence clearly shows how easily readers can become confused and possibly act upon the wrong data or the wrong impression. You might rewrite this sentence to read:

> ***Systems will install the new software by the first of the month so that Human Resources can use it for all new employee applications.***

Look What Others Say About The Passive Voice

In *The Elements of Style*, Strunk and White, discuss the **Active** and **Passive Voice** by saying, "The active voice is usually more direct and vigorous than the passive." They refer to the **Passive Voice** as "less direct, less bold and less concise."

The Publication Manual of the American Psychological Association, Third Edition, says, "Verbs are vigorous, direct communicators. Use the active rather than the passive voice..."

The Gregg Reference Manual, Ninth Edition, states, "Passive verb forms typically produce awkward or stilted sentences."

Mommy and Daddy Need To Party

The AMA Style Guide for Business Writing* from the American Management Association is an excellent resource. It tells us "Use of the active voice is preferable in most writing because it instantly identifies the action with the person who is performing that action. It creates strong, lively writing."

The government publication, ***Plain Letter, Federal Stock Number 7610-00-1091***, also talks about the **Active** and **Passive Voice**. "Another way to strengthen your letters, and at the same time to shorten your sentences, is to use fewer passive verbs and more active ones. The very word passive suggests that too many verbs of this form weaken letters, while the word active suggests that verbs of that form make them stronger." Although this publication is now out of print, the message is clear and powerful. Limit your use of the **Passive Voice**.

For those technically-oriented people, I recommend ***The ACS Styles Guide: A Manual for Authors and Editors***. This book comes from the publishing arm of the American Chemical Society. The ***Foreword*** to the book states, "Our previous handbooks were devoted almost entirely to instruction of contributors to ACS publications in 'the way we do it at ACS.' ...the approach taken here is a more general one, stressing those principles that are desirable throughout the scientific literature." Their style guide clearly says, "Use strong verbs; they are essential to clear, concise writing. Use the active voice whenever possible. It is usually less wordy and unambiguous."

If you know any "techies," let them know about the last paragraph. Most of them traveled through their careers with academic ghosts that required them to write in the **Passive Voice**. Do them a favor. Release them from this bondage.

While I use the above publications to emphasize the importance of the **Active Voice**, I also recommend them as reference tools for other aspects of business writing. You can buy the first three in any reputable book store.

---

* Reprinted from THE AMA STYLE GUIDE FOR BUSINESS WRITING by AMA staff. Copyright © 1996 AMACOM, a division of American Management Association International. Reprinted by permission of AMACOM, a division of American Management Association International, New York, NY. All rights reserved. http:www.amanet.org.

How To Get It Right When You Write

You can order the AMA Style Guide for Business Writing from:

> American Management Association
> 1601 Broadway
> New York, NY 10019-7420
> Telephone: 212-596-8100
> Fax: 212-903-8168

You can order the ACS manual from:

> American Chemical Society
> Distribution Office, Department 225
> 1155 16th Street, N.W.
> Washington, DC 20036
> Telephone: 800-227-5558

The message of these respected authors and publishers suggests **limiting**, not eliminating, the **Passive Voice** from your business writing. The following section discusses times when using the **Passive Voice** becomes practical and sometimes necessary.

Use the Passive Voice When:

1. **The Doer of the action is not known.**

   The bomb was mysteriously placed in the airport locker.

   This example uses the **Passive Voice** in a very logical fashion. Whoever wrote this sentence used the word "mysteriously" to let us know that they did not know who placed the bomb in the locker. Another reason for leaving this in the **Passive Voice** relates again to the **Subject - Verb - Relationship**. Perhaps, the writer truly needed to focus on "the bomb" as the **subject** of the sentence.

   One way the writer might have been able to change this sentence would be to write:

   > *An unknown person placed the bomb in the airport locker.*

   or

   > *Police do not know who placed the bomb in the airport locker.*

Indeed, this sentence now reflects the **Active Voice**. However, to accomplish that, the writer had to use **more** words. This is an exception to the idea of using the **Active Voice** to be more precise and use less words.

Let's try another example.

> **The money was given away.**

This sentence does not state who gave the money away. This could be for several reasons. The writer did not know or did not want to reveal who gave the money away. Or, the information that preceded that sentence may have indicated that this was the wish of some individual. Another possibility might be explained in the next section.

2. **The Doer of the action is not important**.

   He was elected by only three votes.

In this example, who did the electing, or who those three votes were did not matter. If this piece of writing aimed to focus specifically on the candidate, using the **Passive Voice** worked. Using the **Passive Voice** allowed the writer to use "he" as the subject.

The writer still could have used the **Active Voice** to say:

> *He won by only three votes.*

3. **You want to be extremely sensitive or do not want to reveal something.**

   A mistake was made in adding the figures.

This is probably the most common use of the **Passive Voice**. Tact, common sense, and a desire to remain politically correct might prompt the writer to avoid saying:

> *Valerie made an error in adding the figures.*

4. **You use the Passive Voice in a subordinate clause.**

Check back to see how I started this section. I wrote, "Use the **Passive Voice** when:

> **The Doer of the action is not known.**

If I were to write this as a sentence rather than using a bullet format, I might have written that sentence:

> *Use the Passive Voice when the Doer of the action is not known.*

That example uses the **Passive Voice** to state *is not known*. That phrase is in the **Passive Voice**. However, I have used that passive form in the **subordinate clause,** not the **main clause (independent clause)**. The main clause becomes *Use the Passive Voice*. In that clause, we use a concept called "you understood." That means we understand that the subject of the sentence is "you."

If you wrote that sentence out completely it would read:

> *You would use the Passive Voice when the doer of the action is not known.*

Or, in formal writing, you would say:

> *One uses the passive voice when the doer of the action is not known.*

I hope I have not overwhelmed you with this detailed description of the **Active** and **Passive Voice**. My message would be consistent with most writing experts. In business writing, **limit** your use of the **Passive Voice**. Yes, you can use it sometimes. But don't use it constantly as the crutch you once may have to get to **100 Words - 10 Pages - 2 Blue Books**.

I also wanted to offer you enough information so that when your grammar checkers stop you for the **Passive Voice**, you can decide intelligently if, how, or why you might want to change the sentence.

Let's review how you spot the **Passive Voice**.

- The verb of the sentence uses a **Weak Verb** to help a strong verb.
- The subject of the sentence is not performing the action indicated by the verb.
- The person or thing performing the action becomes less important as the object of a preposition at the end of the sentence. Or, as you have just seen, you may not even find the doer of the action mentioned in the sentence.

Mommy and Daddy Need To Party

Practice Changing Passive Voice to Active

Change the following sentences to eliminate the **Passive Voice**, become more graphic and specific, stick to the point, and use less words. Remember, you might need to change or create subjects and even the main verb itself to convey a more powerful message. After you complete this activity, compare your approach to the alternatives or suggestions I offer. Enjoy.

 **YOU NEED A PEN OR PENCIL NOW!**

1. The flowers were delivered by a mysterious lady.

2. The books were soiled by the rain.

3. The problem had been solved by Samantha.

4. A better benefits package was requested by the workers.

5. The results would be seen by the stockholders.

6. This meeting has been called by the Executive Committee.

7. A complaint was lodged by the customer.

8. All new customers will be notified of the procedure changes.

9. This exercise was completed by yours truly.

10. The monthly reports should have been distributed sooner.

Let's Compare Notes

Practice Sentence # 1

> **The flowers were delivered by a mysterious lady.**

The easiest way for you to change this sentence is to say:

> *A mysterious lady delivered the flowers.*

By changing the sentence in this way, you eliminated the words **were** and **by**. This also allowed you to get closer to the eighteen-word average you should strive for and a one-page letter versus a two-page letter. If you wanted to keep *flowers* as the subject of the sentence, you could have said:

> *The flowers came from a mysterious lady.*

The rest of these sentences would follow the same pattern we used above.

Practice Sentence # 2

> **The books were soiled by the rain.**

becomes

> *The rain soiled the books.*

Practice Sentence # 3

> **The problem had been solved by Samantha.**

becomes

> *Samantha solved the problem.*

Practice Sentence # 4

> **A better benefits package was requested by the workers.**

becomes

> *The workers requested a better benefits package.*

Practice Sentence # 5

> **The results would be seen by the stockholders.**

becomes

The stockholders would see the results.

Practice Sentence # 6

This meeting has been called by the Executive Committee.

becomes

The Executive Committee called this meeting.

Practice Sentence # 7

A complaint was lodged by the customer.

becomes

The customer lodged a complaint.

Practice Sentence # 8

All new customers will be notified of the procedure changes.

becomes

Marketing will notify all new customers of the procedure changes.

or

The Communications Department will notify all new customers of the procedure changes.

or

All new customers will receive information about the procedure changes.

Notice in the first two revisions, we changed the subject of the sentence to state *who* will do the notifying. The third revision used the original subject, **All new customers** and changed the verb to **will receive**. Both the original sentence and the revised sentence contain ten words.

Practice Sentence # 9

This exercise was completed by yours truly.

becomes

Hold it! I hope none of you changed this sentence to read:

Yours truly completed this exercise.

Who is this ***yours truly*** person? Get real. People really don't talk that way. Most people would say:

I completed this exercise.

The same way you got rid of ***Yours truly*** in the above sentence should also prompt you to get rid of that phrase as a complimentary close in your letters. If I were to use ***Yours truly*** in business letters, my wife would get very angry with me. I'm truly hers. Most business writing instructors and consultants would recommend ***Sincerely, Best regards***, or ***Regards*** as a substitute.

Practice Sentence # 10

The monthly reports should have been distributed sooner.

This sentence may have caused you problems. You might be asking me, "what's wrong with that sentence?"

I recommend changing this sentence for three reasons. First, this sentence contains the **Passive Voice**. Second, the sentence is too long, and is unclear. Third, it probably would not produce the results you are looking for.

You could have eliminated the **Passive Voice** and made this sentence more specific and shorter by saying:

Distribute the monthly reports sooner.

In that revision, (you) understood becomes the subject of that sentence. Now you have eliminated the **Passive Voice** and became specific in terms of ***who*** should distribute the monthly reports.

You can become more personal and even more specific by saying:

Please distribute the monthly reports by the 15th of each month.

Indeed, you have added three words to the sentence, but you have become more specific and used that great word, ***please***.

You could also change the sentence to read:

> ***Information systems should have distributed the monthly reports sooner.***

or

> ***Accounting should have distributed the monthly reports sooner.***

or

> ***The mail room should have distributed the monthly reports sooner.***

In these revisions, you now state who should have delivered the reports sooner. Sooner or later, someone will ask you, "Who is responsible for the reports being late?"

Let's get practical. The original sentence, ***The monthly reports should have been distributed sooner,*** would probably not produce the results you were looking for. Probably, the reader would read the sentence and think "Yes, you're right" and move on.

Why would **you** write a sentence like that? What you probably think and mean is:

> ***I need the monthly reports sooner.***

Being more specific, you would write:

> ***I need the monthly reports by the 15th of each month.***

Now you have conveyed a reason and a sense of urgency to your readers. What people think and what they say can be two different things. What people think and what they write can be two different things. Business writing requires you to convey exactly what you think clearly on paper.

Avoid Nowhere Adverbs

Nowhere Adverbs are those constructions in American business writing that start with the adverb, *there* and add a **Weak Verb**. For example, *there are*, *there is*, *there could have been*, *there should have been.* **Nowhere Adverbs** affect your writing in four ways.

Nowhere Adverbs:

- Force you to use Weak Verbs.

- Cloud the Subject.

- Add no value or impact to the sentence.

- Force you to use longer sentences.

Let's look at an example of how **Nowhere Adverbs** weaken your writing and add length but not strength.

There are many things you must learn before you are promoted.

In the above example, the first word of that sentence is *there*. When I say the *there*, what is the first thing that comes to your mind? 99.99% of the people in my workshops respond loudly, **"Where?"** Does the example sentence tell you where anything is? No.

The second word in the sentence is *are*. *Are* is a **Weak Verb**. You have two feet in the grave and you haven't started the sentence.

In the above example sentence, please circle the subject of that sentence.

When I do this in my seminars, participants normally offer as subjects of that sentence *there* and *you*. Technically speaking, the subject of that sentence becomes *things*.

I suggested earlier in the book that every time you use a **Weak Verb** you tend to cloud the subject. This sentence is a typical example of that.

 **YOU NEED A PEN OR PENCIL NOW!**

In the text box below, write how you would change the example sentence to eliminate the **Nowhere Adverb**, *there* plus a **Weak Verb**, and use the remaining words in that sentence.

You could have changed the sentence in two ways.

> *You must learn many things before you are promoted.*

or

> *Before you are promoted, you must learn many things.*

Either way you do this, you have:

- Shortened the sentence.
- Used a strong verb.
- Become more specific because people now know *who* is doing *what.*

Also now, if I asked you to find the subject in either of the two suggested changes, I'm sure you would spot *you* as the subject of both sentences.

Every once in a while, a seminar participant will change that sentence to read.

> *Many things must be learned before you are promoted.*

Let's examine this sentence to determine its impact. Let's pretend that Brian is my boss. Brian and I are in Brian's office discussing my annual performance review. Brian concludes the meeting by reading to me the last sentence on my appraisal form:

> *Many things must be learned before you are promoted.*

I would jump up, shake Brian's hand, thank him and assure him that would happen. I would then leave Brian's office and run to Chris's office and urgently announce to her, "Chris, you've got to learn a lot of things. I want to get promoted."

When Brian said to me, **"Many things must be learned before you are promoted,"** he did not say *I* had to learn them. Therefore, I'm going to dump the responsibility on someone else.

Some of you might think the above scenario was comical. The sad part about this whole situation is that this example of miscommunication happens thousands of times every day in the business world.

Let's examine another example of a **Nowhere Adverb**.

> **If there is an Al Borowski in the building, please report to the main lobby.**

This is an example of a sentence I once heard over a company intercom. Please understand what that sentence means. That means because I am in the building, everyone else in the building must report to the main lobby.

The subject of that sentence is *you* understood. To clearly show what that sentence says or to find out what the subject is, read only the part of the sentence after the comma.

> *Please report to the main lobby.*

If you read only that much, you can see that this sentence requests *you* to report to the lobby.

Notice also, in the original example, the writer turned me into a **thing**. The sentence uses the phrase, *"an* Al Borowski." This sentence is an example of the depersonalization conspiracy in business writing. The sentence should have read:

> *Al Borowski, please report to the main lobby.*

Sometimes, eliminating **Nowhere Adverbs** can be as simple as eliminating the **Nowhere Adverb**. Check this sentence.

> **We discovered there was a rocket in the storage area.**

Mommy and Daddy Need To Party

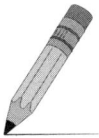 **YOU NEED A PEN OR PENCIL NOW!**

With your pen or pencil, cross out the words, ***there was***. The sentence now reads:

We discovered a rocket in the storage area.

Magic! You eliminated two words that carried absolutely, positively no value or power. Why were those two words in that sentence? You know — **100 Words - 10 Pages - 2 Blue Books. Big People Like Big Words - Big People Like Big Sentences**.

And you made the sentence clearer. Think about the **Subject - Verb - Relationship**. Reading the first four words of the original and revised versions shows the power of clear writing.

We discovered there was…

We discovered a rocket…

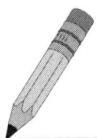 **YOU NEED A PEN OR PENCIL NOW!**

Let's try a few more examples of **Nowhere Adverbs**.

There is reason to suspect that low morale, wage freezes, and indiscriminate firings will prompt a union vote.

The easiest way to change this sentence is to **draw a line** through the first six words. Go ahead, use your pen or pencil to wipe them out. You will find that activity therapeutic and useful. That action of crossing out words on paper should now become a habit. It should become part of your normal routine when you write.

The sentence should now read:

Low morale, wage freezes, and indiscriminate firings will prompt a union vote.

How To Get It Right When You Write

If you are a researcher or an analyst or if your job requires digging up facts, you can write the sentence above. If you are not sure, you can then use "hedge" words like ***may** prompt*, ***could** prompt*, ***might** prompt*. Some of you may have changed the sentence using these "hedge" words because you focused on the word ***suspect**.*

In the original sentence, ***reason*** became the subject of the sentence. In the corrected version, you now have a compound subject, ***low morale, wage freezes, and indiscriminate firings***.

Let's review what we have done with this sentence.

- We have eliminated a **Nowhere Adverb** and six words.
- We made the sentence clearer by sticking to the subject.
- We created a more vivid picture by using a strong verb that showed a clear relationship.

Let's look at the sample sentence in another way. In changing that sentence, some of you focused on the word ***suspect***. Think about it. What does that sentence really mean? What should the author have really written? That sentence should have read:

> *I suspect low morale, wage freezes and indiscriminate firings will prompt a union vote.*

Write what you mean and mean what you write. Why did the author use the **Nowhere Adverb**? Probably the answer lies in a little voice that said, ***Never start a sentence with "I."***

Now you see why we started using **Nowhere Adverbs**. We needed a way to get around the completely non-existent rules about starting a sentence with "I" or using "I" in business letters. So, rather than saying, ***I suspect***, we came up with ***there is reason to suspect that***.

Also, this technique definitely helped us get to **100 Words - 10 Pages - 2 Blue Books. Big People Like Big Words - Big People Like Big Sentences**.

You could have also changed this sentence to read:

> *A union vote normally follows low morale, wage freezes, and indiscriminate firings.*

Doing so, you change the subject of the sentence to focus on the union vote. Remember, you have complete control over the **Subject - Verb - Relationship**. That also carries the responsibility to write clear concise sentences.

Now watch what happens with this next sentence.

> **With this situation, there is involved an apparent reorganization of all 15 departments in the company.**

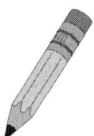 **YOU NEED A PEN OR PENCIL NOW!**

Before you read my suggestions on changing this sentence, find your pen or pencil.

In the above sample sentence, please circle the following words: *Situation*, *reorganization*, *departments*, *company*. While you still have your pen or pencil in your hand, cross out the **Nowhere Adverb**, *there is*. To do that, you need to go all the way back to the beginning of the sentence and cross out the preposition *with*. And, you need to cross out the *comma*. The sentence now reads:

> *This situation involved an apparent reorganization of all 15 departments in the company.*

Let's analyze what this means to you. First, you wiped out a **Nowhere Adverb**, thereby eliminating three needless words and the typing space required for the comma. Second, you clearly positioned your **Subject-Verb-Relationship**. Third, you used less words and said much more.

Now let me tell you why I asked you to circle those four words in the sentence. You can use any one of those four words as the subject of your sentence. You could say:

> *This situation involved an apparent reorganization of all 15 departments in the company.*

or

> *This reorganization involved all 15 departments in the company.*

or

All 15 departments in the company reorganized.

or

The company reorganized all 15 departments.

or

The company reorganized all departments.

Before we leave **Nowhere Adverbs**, let's recall what they are and what they do.

Nowhere Adverbs:

- Force you to use Weak Verbs.
- Cloud the Subject.
- Add no value or impact to the sentence.
- Force you to use longer sentences.

Practice Eliminating Nowhere Adverbs

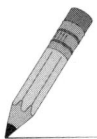 **YOU NEED A PEN OR PENCIL NOW!**

Change the following sentences to eliminate the **Nowhere Adverbs**, become more graphic and specific, stick to the point, and use less words. Remember, you might need to change or create subjects and even the main verb itself to convey a more powerful message. After you complete this activity, compare your approach to the task to the alternatives or suggestions I offer. Enjoy.

1. There is an important vote that will reach the floor of the Senate today.

2. There are several items listed below that we would like you to respond to.

3. There is no special formula for making me happy.

4. Lydia acknowledged there is a great need to eliminate labels such as "masculine" and "feminine."

5. There are many reasons why you should review his report.

6. We discovered there were special circumstances in her situation.

7. Make sure there is enough toner in the copier.

8. There had been several instances reported by the accounting department of fraud within the bank.

9. There seems to be some confusion about your report.

10. If there is anything I can do for you, please call me.

Let's Compare Notes

 **YOU NEED A PEN OR PENCIL NOW!**

Practice Sentence # 1

> There is an important vote that will reach the floor of the Senate today.

In the sample sentence, draw a line through the words, *There is*, and *that*. The sentence now reads

> *An important vote will reach the floor of the Senate today.*

By eliminating those three words, you

1. used less words.
2. used a **Strong Verb**, *will reach*, rather than the **Weak Verb**, *is*.
3. turned a complex sentence into a simple sentence.
4. brought the **Subject** of the sentence closer to the beginning for more impact.
5. made the sentence clearer.

Practice Sentence # 2

> There are several items listed below that we would like you to respond to.

In **Sample Sentence # 2**, you find the **Nowhere Adverb** as the first two words of the sentence. Earlier in the book, you learned that you can end a sentence with a preposition. This practice sentence ends with a preposition. Starting the sentence with the **Nowhere Adverb** forced you to use more words.

You could have said:

> *We would like you to respond to the items listed below.*

or

Please respond to the items listed below.

or

To help speed up the application process, please respond to the items listed below.

Although the last example contains more words, it offers the reader a reason why the authors request the information. Sometimes you need to sacrifice your conciseness to become clear.

Practice Sentence # 3

There is no special formula for making me happy.

You could have changed this sentence to read:

No special formula makes me happy.

or

Making me happy requires no special formula.

or

My happiness needs no special formula.

or

I am easy to please.

Practice Sentence # 4

Lydia acknowledged there is a great need to eliminate labels such as "masculine" and "feminine."

The easiest way to change this sentence is to simply eliminate the **Nowhere Adverb**, *there is*. The sentence now reads:

Lydia acknowledged a great need to eliminate labels such as "masculine" and "feminine."

Those two words, *there is*, add absolutely no power or value to that sentence. Actually, they weaken the sentence.

The sentence does use a strong verb. The subject of this sentence is clear — Lydia. But, notice how the sentence becomes weaker using the **Nowhere Adverb**, *there is.*

Read the sentence out loud. You will see where and how readers would pause.

>Lydia acknowledged there is…

>Lydia acknowledged a great need…

What did she acknowledge? She acknowledged *a great need*, not a *there is*.

Practice Sentence # 5

>**There are many reasons why you should review his report.**

You could change this sentence several ways:

>*You should review his report for many reasons.*

>or

>*His report requires your careful review.*

>or

>*Many parts of his report call for your careful review.*

>or

>*I suggest you read Section Three of his report.*

>or

>*Section Three of his report involves a commitment from your department.*

Write what you mean and mean what you write. You control the **Subject - Verb - Relationship**. You become clear and specific by focusing on what you write as the subject and how it relates to the rest of the sentence.

Practice Sentence # 6

>**We discovered there were special circumstances in her situation.**

Again, the easiest way to shorten this sentence and become more specific and focused simply requires you to remove the **Nowhere Adverb**, *there were*. The sentence would then read:

> *We discovered special circumstances in her situation.*

or

> *We discovered her situation required special attention.*

or

> *Special circumstances required us to review her situation.*

Each way you change the sentence, it becomes shorter and more specific. Notice also, that you might change the meaning or intent of the sentence.

Practice Sentence # 7

> **Make sure there is enough toner in the copier.**

You could change this sentence to read:

> *Make sure enough toner is in the copier.*

or

> *Make sure the copier contains enough toner.*

or

> *The copier may need toner.*

or

> *The copier needs more toner.*

or

> *Please check the amount of toner in the copier.*

You get the idea?

Practice Sentence # 8

> **There had been several instances reported by the accounting department of fraud within the bank.**

This could read:

> *The bank experienced several instances of fraud according to the accounting department.*

or

The accounting department reported several instances of fraud within the bank.

Become creative or maybe more focused and specific.

Fraud within the bank has become a major issue for management.

Practice Sentence # 9

There seems to be some confusion about your report.

Let's analyze what this sentence is trying to say. Where is the confusion? Who is confused? Why is the writer mentioning this? Does the confusion exist about parts of the report or the existence of the report in the first place? The real confusion centers around the intent of the writer.

Perhaps the writer really meant:

I'm confused by your report.

or

I'm confused by certain parts of your report.

or

I'm confused by the focus of your report.

or

I'm confused by the format of your report.

or

I need help understanding parts of your report.

I know. I know. You were terrified of starting a sentence with *I* and using contractions. But, do you notice how starting with *I* helps avoid blaming the other person or the report? Using *I* allows you to take a more personal approach to the situation.

Otherwise, you would change the sentence to read:

Your report confuses me.

or

Parts of your report confuse me.

or

Parts of your report are confusing.

or

You need to redo parts of your report.

Practice Sentence # 10

If there is anything I can do for you, please call me.

Remember, the primary goal of this activity is to eliminate **Nowhere Adverbs**. Thus, the easiest way to change this sentence is to eliminate the **Nowhere Adverb**, *there is* and rearrange the remaining words.

If I can do anything for you, please call me.

You can also express the same message, intent or attitude by saying:

Please let me know what else I can do for you.

A lot of people get nervous suggesting that they can *help* people in any way. They feel that they may offend the person by using the word *help*. Therefore, they would write something like:

Please let me know if I can be of any assistance.

Get real. Do you really think your readers are that transparent that they don't know the difference or that they see a big difference in the words *help* and *assistance*. If you do feel that way, I suggest you take the heat off yourself and your readers and simply say:

I will call you next week to follow up.

Now you have taken the responsibility of making the call rather than forcing your readers to take action. Tell me how you feel. Call me; write me; fax me; e-mail me. I am interested in your comments on this subject.

Avoid Artificial Antecedents

I created the phrase **Artificial Antecedent** as an exaggerated way to alert people of a writing habit or technique they need to be aware of. An **Artificial Antecedent** is a combination of words that added no value or power to your writing but allowed you to compile **100 Words - 10 Pages - 2 Blue Books** or to avoid using the personal pronoun *I*.

Later, when you become comfortable that you can recognize and correct **Artificial Antecedents**, you will probably call this construction *The It Thing*. You will learn why soon.

To explain **Artificial Antecedents**, I must use a three-step approach. We will discuss:

Antecedents	What are they and why are they important?
Incorrect antecedents	How do they affect your writing?
Artificial Antecedents	What are they and why are they important?

Before we talk about **Artificial Antecedents**, we need to discuss antecedents. Before we talk about antecedents, let's talk about something a little easier. Can you all remember *pronouns*? Pronouns are those little words that take the place of nouns.

Let's look at the following example:

Jimmy found a ball and took it home.

In the above sentence, the pronoun becomes *it*. Remember these personal pronouns *I, me, you, he, she, it, they*. An *antecedent* is the noun to which the pronoun refers. So, in our sample sentence, *it* is the pronoun and *ball* becomes the antecedent. *It* and *ball* mean the same thing. This sentence is an example of a *correct antecedent*.

Now consider this sentence:

Jimmy found a ball in the field and took it home.

In this sentence, *it,* remains as the pronoun. However, this sentence contains an incorrect or unclear antecedent. If this sentence were grammatically and technically correct, Jimmy's mom would be awfully upset. According to this sentence, Jimmy took *the field* home. I don't think that was the intent of this sentence.

You can correct this sentence several ways. You can eliminate the prepositional phrase *in the field* to turn the sentence into our original example.

Jimmy found a ball and took it home.

If, **where** he found *the ball* is important, you could write:

In the field, Jimmy found a ball and took it home.

Now you know *the ball* is going home, not *the field*. To do this you had to add one typing space for the comma. This is an instance where I recommend sacrificing your conciseness to make the sentence clearer.

You could have also written:

Jimmy found a ball in the field and took the ball home.

Some of you have creepy crawlies all over your body. Some of you are now ready to call me, write me, fax me, or e-mail me. Horror of horrors, Borowski!!!

"You used the same word twice in the same sentence. The grammar police will get you!"

Let's talk about this. Yes, you can use the same word twice in the same sentence. When I said, "Jimmy found a ball in the field and took the ball home," I'm sure all of you knew what was going home. This is another example of where I recommend sacrificing your conciseness to become clearer. In that new example, I added seven typing spaces. Those seven typing spaces made the sentence clear, specific, and accurate.

Some of you are now angry with me because you think I am insulting your intelligence. I know what you are thinking. When you use the sentence "Jimmy found a ball in the field and took it home," we all know he isn't taking the *field* home.

I use that example because I do not want anyone to assume anything. When you say that people will know "Jimmy is not taking the field home," you may be correct. I used exaggeration when I called these constructions **Artificial Antecedents**. I also used exaggeration when I used the word *field* in the sample sentence. I wanted you to get a mental picture of Jimmy trying to take a field home. We know that is impossible.

Remember, I was trying to show an example of an incorrect or unclear antecedent. Suppose I used the example:

> ***Jimmy found the ball in the bucket and took it home.***

Now what's going home? The ball, the bucket, or both?

So far, we have talked about *correct antecedents* and *incorrect antecedents*. We still haven't talked about **Artificial Antecedents**. I know that you don't use **Artificial Antecedents**. But, your bosses do. I know all of you have received a letter, memo, or report that started:

> **It has come to my attention...**
> **It is important that...**
> **It is with indescribable joy that I announce...**

Each of those three sentences starts with the pronoun *it.* What is the antecedent of *It*? You don't know. It doesn't exist. It's imaginary. It's artificial.

Let me explain what **Artificial Antecedents** are, how they affect your writing, and what you can do about it.

Artificial Antecedents start with the pronoun *it,* and add a **Weak Verb** or the **Passive Voice** to create a construction that makes a sentence longer, more confusing and less personal.

Let me explain how this works. Consider the example:

 **YOU NEED A PEN OR PENCIL NOW!**

> **It is obvious that the Hinkle Dinkle Manufacturing Company hires the best people.**

Mommy and Daddy Need To Party

Please circle the **subject** of the example sentence. Most participants in my seminars circle *Hinkle Dinkle Manufacturing Company*. Technically or grammatically, the subject of that sentence is *it*.

Remember our discussion about how the use of **Weak Verbs** and needless words **cloud** the subject of the sentence. This example clearly shows what that means and how it happens. Notice also that the verb in that sentence becomes *is*.

What should be the subject of that sentence? – the **Hinkle Dinkle Manufacturing Company**.

Now, draw a line through the first four words of the sample sentence. The sentence now reads:

The Hinkle Dinkle Manufacturing Company hires the best people.

Wiping out those four words leaves the *Hinkle Dinkle Manufacturing Company* as the **subject** of the sentence and allows you to use *hires* as the **strong verb**. The four words you wiped out had no power and no value.

Why would anyone write a sentence using four words that contribute nothing to the sentence? You know. **100 Words - 10 Pages - 2 Blue Books. Big People Like Big Words - Big People Like Big Sentences**.

What else could you use as the subject of the sentence? Right! **Best people**.

 **YOU NEED A PEN OR PENCIL NOW!**

In the text box that follows, change the sample sentence to use **best people** as the subject of the sentence.

In my workshops, 99.99% of the participants change this to:

> *The best people are hired by the Hinkle Dinkle Manufacturing Company.*

How To Get It Right When You Write

If you did that, go back to the sentence you wrote or the sentence the way the participants change it and circle the words, *are* and *by*. These two words remind you that you slipped back into the **Passive Voice**. Who did the hiring? HDMC. Where do you find HDMC? Way at the end of the sentence as the object of the preposition, *by*.

To stay in the **Active Voice**, maintain the correct **Subject - Verb - Relationship**, and use less words you would probably write:

> *The best people work for the Hinkle Dinkle Manufacturing Company.*

 **YOU NEED A PEN OR PENCIL NOW!**

Let's try a few more samples.

> **In a report to the company president, it was disclosed that profits were low and costs of sales were high.**

With this sentence, your objective is to eliminate the **Artificial Antecedent**, make the sentence clearer and more concise.

In the sample sentence above, cross out the words *it was*. Now, cross out the preposition *in*. And, cross out the **comma**.

The sentence now reads:

> *A report to the company president disclosed that profits were low and costs of sales were high.*

Now cross out the word *that*.

> *A report to the company president disclosed profits were low and costs of sales were high.*

Now cross out the **Weak Verbs**, *were,* and *were,* and rearrange the rest of the words in the sentence to read:

> *A report to the company president disclosed low profits and high costs of sales.*

Now cross out the preposition, *of,* and rearrange the rest of the words in the sentence to read:

> ***A report to the company president disclosed low profits and high sales costs.***

Important Note

Remember, in business writing, you must always focus on your purpose and your audience. If your audience for the last example sentence were accountants or financial people, you would leave the word *of* in the sentence.

The phrases *cost of sales* and *sales costs* mean two completely different things to accountants and financial people. That's why you must focus on your audience.

The next sample sentence carries a lot of baggage with it.

> **It has been found that lack of parking, high prices, poor service, and limited selection drive customers away.**

To eliminate the **Artificial Antecedent** in this sentence, you would cross out the first five words. The sentence now reads:

> *Lack of parking, high prices, poor service, and limited selection drive customers away.*

The **Artificial Antecedents**, *it has been found* contains the pronoun *it* followed by the **Passive Voice** phrase *has been found*. Perhaps, whoever did the *finding* is important to the meaning of the sentence. So, you might write:

> ***Government studies show lack of parking, high prices, poor service, and limited selection drive customers away.***

or

> *A Grocery Association's market research tells us lack of parking, high prices, poor service, and limited selection drive customers away.*

If you wanted to use *customers* as the subject of the sentence, you would write:

> *Customers avoid stores with lack of parking, high prices, poor service, and limited selection.*

All of the above example sentences reflect a negative tone. We can turn the tone positive by saying:

> *Customers look for ample parking, low prices, excellent service, and a varied selection.*

or

> *Customers generally shop stores with ample parking, low prices, excellent service, and a varied selection.*

or

> *Government studies show ample parking, low prices, excellent service, and a varied selection attract customers.*

Let's try one final example that clearly shows that people should write the way they talk.

> **It is therefore incumbent upon all employees to put forth their best efforts to overcome the minor problems that beset our company.**

This sentence may create a challenge for some of you. If you attempted to change it, I applaud you. I am sure you eliminated the **Artificial Antecedent**, *it is therefore incumbent upon,* and shortened the sentence.

Before I share with you the way I would change this sentence, let me ask a couple of questions. What kind of person or what level of person would be inclined to write a sentence like the above example?

Most of my workshops participants agree that a sentence with a message like the example sentence would most likely be a high level person in an organization. That person would probably be a CEO, President, Vice President, or Senior Officer. Now, I would like to place you in two situations.

In the first situation, you come home from work to find a letter or telegram that contains the sentence, "It is therefore incumbent upon all employees to put forth their best efforts to overcome the minor problems that beset our company."

In the second situation, the sentence reads:

I ask you to help us get through these difficult times.

Which sentence would produce positive results for the writer? Again, workshop participants agree. The second sentence, with the simple language and personal tone, would bring better results. The more you take a personal approach towards your audience, the better your chances of getting positive results.

Let's review **Artificial Antecedents** or, if you prefer, the **It Thing**.

An **Artificial Antecedent** combines the pronoun, *it* with either a **Weak Verb** or the **Passive Voice**.

For example:

> It is important that…
>
> It is obvious that…
>
> It has been found…
>
> It has been stated…

The following page contains a partial list of **Artificial Antecedents**, or if you prefer, the **It Thing** that I have compiled. I have a list of at least 125 more sitting in my computer. Space limited putting the complete list in this book.

Special note:

This copyrighted list took years to compile. I trust that software companies will respect my copyright and not include them in their versions of grammar checkers.

This list exists solely for the use of writers who attend my workshops or buy my books, tapes, videos and CD's.

Artificial Antecedents

As it can be seen	It is expected that
As it was explained to you	It is hoped to
It has come to my attention	It is our practice
It is important that	It is procedure
It is obvious that	It is relatively easy
It is with a great deal of pride that	It would be advantageous
It is with indescribable joy that	It will help her if
It occurred to me that the	It is my impression
It is annoying when	It was determined
As it stands now	It would be difficult
It is our policy	It becomes apparent
It is our plan	It may be necessary
It is possible	It is learned
It doesn't matter	It is unclear
It's amazing	It was felt
It never ceases to amaze me	It was discovered
It's just like her	It is important to note
It's cold in here	It is helpful to
It's in your best interest	It is my belief
It's up to you	It was evident
It makes good sense	It is well-known
It may be	It's hard to believe
It was reported	It is clear that
It was my concern	It is in the best interest of
It concerns me	It is acceptable
It might be suitable	It's all gone
It was a pleasure	It never fails
It appears	It is a responsibility of

Artificial Antecedents

It has been a pleasure	It should make sense
It would be possible	It would be in your best interest
It would be most advantageous	It is easy to see
It seems	It is too early to tell
It will no longer be necessary	It's nice to hear from you
It is a great pleasure	It may take time
If it is determined	It might be helpful
It sounds like	It looks like
It would be good	It is strongly recommended
It is critical	It is absolutely critical
It is nice	It happens that
It is not fully understood	It is important to note
It may have been a mistake	It is encouraging
It is our role	It is quite possible
It is essential	It is a necessary part of
It is imperative that	It is a necessity of
It is unwise	It has been confirmed
It seems as though	It would be difficult to say
It's my job	It had not been known that long
It is up to me	It is highly unlikely
It gives me satisfaction	She takes it upon herself
It took time	When it gets busy around here

Practice Eliminating Artificial Antecedents

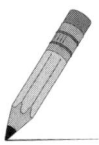 **YOU NEED A PEN OR PENCIL NOW!**

Change the following sentences to eliminate **Artificial Antecedents**, become more graphic and specific, stick to the point, and use less words. Remember, you might need to change or create subjects and even the main verb itself to convey a more powerful message. After you complete this activity, compare your approach to the task to the alternatives or suggestions I offer. Enjoy.

1. Company policy states that it is the responsibility of all employees to report all accidents the day the accidents occur.

2. Until it has been confirmed that all employee discounts will be increased to 20%, please continue to use the previously established 15% figure.

3. It seems likely that the recent additions to our staff will eliminate the bottlenecks caused in customer service.

4. We feel it should be noted that 12 employees won prizes in the recent promotion.

5. The captain will let us know when it is safe to stand.

6. It was a pleasure meeting you at the national convention.

7. It was confirmed during the audit that several thousand dollars showed up missing.

8. It has been suggested that you resign.

9. We feel it is very important to keep all managers informed about the procedural changes when they impact government regulations.

10. "It was a day like no other."

Let's Compare Notes

 **YOU NEED A PEN OR PENCIL NOW!**

Practice Sentence # 1

Company policy states that it is the responsibility of all employees to report all accidents the day the accidents occur.

With this sentence, your objective was to eliminate the **Artificial Antecedents**, make the sentence clearer and more concise.

In the practice sentence above, cross out the words *it is the responsibility of* and *to*. Now, add the word *must* after the *employees*.

The sentence now reads:

Company policy states that employees must report all accidents the day the accidents occur.

Actually, the sentence would probably read better as:

Company policy states that employees who are involved in work-related accidents must report them the day the accidents occur.

Although this sentence is longer, it becomes clearer and more specific. The original and the revised versions could cause some confusion. Both imply *all* employees must report the accidents, even if they were not involved.

Practice Sentence # 2

Until it has been confirmed that all employees discounts will be increased to 20%, please continue to use the previously established 15% figure.

To eliminate the **Artificial Antecedents** in this sentence, you would cross out *it has been* and add *we confirm* or *we have confirmed*.

Besides eliminating the **Artificial Antecedent**, you have eliminated the **Passive Voice**. Now the employees know **who** will confirm the information.

This sentence now reads:

> **Until we confirm that all employee discounts will be increased to 20%, please continue to use the previously established 15% figure.**

Practice Sentence # 3

> **It seems likely that the recent additions to our staff will eliminate the bottlenecks caused in customer service.**

The fastest and easiest way to change this sentence is to eliminate the **Artificial Antecedent** *it seems likely that*. The sentence now reads:

> ***The recent additions to our staff will eliminate the bottlenecks caused in customer service.***

You can shorten the sentence even more by eliminating the words *the, to, our, the, caused,* and *in*. The sentence now reads:

> ***Recent staff additions will eliminate customer service bottlenecks.***

or

> ***Recent staff additions may eliminate customer service bottlenecks.***

or

> ***Recent staff additions should eliminate customer service bottlenecks.***

Practice Sentence # 4

> **We feel it should be noted that 12 employees won prizes in the recent promotion.**

In that sentence, *it should be noted* appears as the **Artificial Antecedent**.

The questions arise – What is *it*? And, ***noted by whom***?

You can eliminate the **Artificial Antecedent** and use less words by changing the sentence to read:

> ***We feel you should know that 12 employees won prizes in the recent promotion.***

or

> *We should note that 12 employees won prizes in the recent promotion.*

or

> *We feel honored that 12 employees won prizes in the recent promotion.*

Perhaps all you need to say is:

> *Twelve employees won prizes in the recent promotion.*

Practice Sentence # 5

The captain will let us know when it is safe to stand.

The sentence should read:

> ***The captain will let us know when we can safely stand.***

Notice in the original sentence, the writer used the personal pronoun, *us*. I guess personal pronoun paranoia struck after using that first pronoun and the writer became terrified of using two in one sentence. That might anger the twin gods of **Repetition** and **Personal References**.

Actually, the sentence should say:

> ***The captain will let you know when you may safely stand and retrieve your carry-on items.***

Practice Sentence # 6

It was a pleasure meeting you at the national convention.

Eliminating the **Artificial Antecedent** in this sentence means changing the sentence to read:

> ***I enjoyed meeting you at the national convention.***

I truly believe this is what people mean when they say, "It was a pleasure meeting you at the national convention." People use this sentence because they are terrified of starting a sentence with the personal pronoun *I*. Because of this terror, they created an awkward construction that de-personalized the message and made the sentence longer. They also used this awkward construction because of habit. We started using these constructions to help us get to **100 Words - 10 Pages - 2 Blue Books. Big People like Big Words - Big People Like Big Sentences**.

Practice Sentence # 7

> **It was confirmed during the audit that several thousand dollars showed up missing.**

You can rid this sentence of the **Artificial Antecedent**, *it was confirmed* several ways. You could write:

> *The audit confirmed that several thousand dollars showed up missing.*

or

> *The accounting department confirmed that the audit found several thousand dollars missing.*

or

> *The auditors found several thousand dollars missing.*

or

> *The audit found several thousand dollars missing.*

or

> *The Accounting Department reported several thousand dollars missing.*

Let's not forget:

> *Several thousand dollars showed up missing in the audit.*

Practice Sentence # 8

> **It has been suggested that you resign.**

If you got home from work and found a letter or telegram that contained the above sentence, what would be the first question you would ask? Most people would want to know, **"Who suggested that I resign?"** Give them the answer.

> *I suggest you resign.*

or

The board suggests you resign.

or

Your manager suggests you resign.

or

Your workers suggest you resign.

Remember, one of our goals with this book is to save you time. If you use the original sentence, you may need to spend additional time explaining the *who* or *why* of that sentence later.

Practice Sentence # 9

We feel it is very important to keep all managers informed about the procedural changes when they impact government regulations.

Again, you have several ways to change this sentence.

Please keep all managers informed about the procedural changes when they impact government regulations.

or

We ask you to keep all managers informed about the procedural changes when they impact government regulations.

or

Managers need current information about procedural changes when they impact government regulations.

Practice Sentence # 10

"It was a day like no other."

I hope none of you changed this sentence. Notice that the sentence is in quotation marks. This sentence is the opening line of a book and the opening line of a movie. The movie starred Kathleen Turner, Michael Douglas and Danny DeVito. The movie was *Jewel of the Nile*.

This sentence, however, brings out an important point about the difference between business writing and literature. If you are writing a novel, a short story, a screen play or a poem, you have time to develop characters, build scenery, and create suspense. When you write a letter, memo, report, e-mail or proposal, you don't have this time.

Avoid Turning Strong Verbs Into Nouns Or Adjectives

The fifth way people misuse verbs involves turning good, strong verbs into nouns or adjectives. This happens when you add *ion, tion, ation, al, ment, sis* or *ive* onto a strong verb. For example, consider the following sentence:

Flowers are a reflection of our deepest feelings.

Notice the following points in that sentence.

1. The sentence contains the **Weak Verb** *are.*
2. The sentence contains the word *reflection.*
3. The sentence contains eight words.

Okay. In the sample sentence, cross out *are, a, ion,* and *of.*
Read what's left.

Flowers reflect our deepest feelings.

Now:

1. The sentence uses the strong verb *"reflect."*
2. The sentence creates a more vivid picture.
3. The sentence contains only five words.

Any time you add *ion, tion, ation, al, ment, sis* or *ive* to a strong verb, you must then use a **Weak Verb**.

Let's try a few more examples.

This memo is in recognition of his accomplishments.

In that sample sentence, notice the word, *recognition.* It ends in *ion.* Also notice the **Weak Verb** *is*. And, notice the preposition *of*. Those three items together in a sentence offer a clue you might be able to change the sentence to become more clear, concise, correct, complete, and conversational. The revised sentence would read:

This memo recognizes his accomplishments.

Here's another example:

His answer was indicative of his attitude toward new employees.

You can eliminate two words by changing *was indicative of* to *indicated* or *reflected* or even *displayed*.

His answer indicated his attitude toward new employees.

or

His answer reflected his attitude toward new employees.

or

His answer displayed his attitude toward new employees.

Changing the sentence that way used two less words and eight less spaces. Glance at both of those sentences. Notice how long your eyes must stay on the first example to capture the full meaning of the words. Now look how quickly and easily your eyes capture the message in the revised versions.

How would you change the following?

1. We are of the opinion…
2. They are in agreement…
3. I am hesitant to…
4. Our manager gave approval to…
5. He is appreciative of…

Great job. I knew you would catch on quickly. I believe you would have said:

1. We think…
2. They agree…

3. I hesitate to…

4. Our manager approved…

5. He appreciates…

Please notice three important writing issues.

First, you changed four words, **are of the opinion** to *think*. The word **opinion** in that sentence is a noun.

Second, examples 2 and 4 contain the nouns **agreement** and **approval**, that you changed back into strong verbs.

Third, example 3 and 5 contained the adjectives **hesitate** and **appreciate** that you changed back into strong verbs.

Now you understand what happens when you use *ion*, *tion*, *ation*, *al*, *ment*, *sis* or *ive* at the end of a strong verb. Doing so forces you to use a **Weak Verb**, add more typing spaces, and sometimes more words.

Practice Changing Nouns Back Into Strong Verbs

 **YOU NEED A PEN OR PENCIL NOW!**

Change the following sentences that contain **verbs that became nouns** to use a strong verb, become more graphic, and specific, stick to the point, and use less words. Remember, you might need to change or create subjects and even the main verb itself to convey a more powerful message. After you complete this activity, turn the page and compare your approach to the alternatives or suggestions I offer. Enjoy.

1. Our manager made a recommendation that we sell the returned goods for half price.

2. Containment of the flames was done quickly by the fire fighters.

3. Special orders cause complications in the scheduling system.

4. Todd gave a refusal on the plan to build a new prototype.

5. The lab took an analysis of the sample.

6. The board arrived at a determination that the policy needed an overhaul.

7. Please make a notation of your selection on the enclosed form.

8. After you have reviewed the enclosed material, please give consideration to becoming a sponsor for this program.

9. Engineering made modifications to the galootin pin.

10. I am appreciative of all your help.

Let's Compare Notes

Practice Sentence # 1

> **Our manager made a recommendation that we sell the returned goods for half price.**

Remember, in this activity, we are trying to eliminate verbs that became nouns by adding ***ion, ation, al, ment, sis or ire***. The practice sentence contains the noun, *recommendation*. This noun comes from the strong verb, *recommend*.

When you think of the verb, *make,* what mental picture do you get? Normally, you would think of an ounce of "this" a dash of "that," and a sprinkle of something else to make your favorite recipe. Or, attach bolt "A" to nut "B" and clamp on brace "C" to *make* something.

Change this sentence to read:

> ***Our manager recommended we sell the returned goods for half price.***

Did the manager make anything? No. What did the manager do? He or she *recommended*. Give people credit for what they do.

Practice Sentence # 2

> **Containment of the flames was done quickly by the fire fighters.**

becomes

> ***The fire fighters quickly contained the flames.***

Practice Sentence # 3

> **Special orders cause complications in the scheduling system.**

becomes

> ***Special orders complicate the scheduling system.***

Practice Sentence # 4

> **Todd gave a refusal on the plan to build a new prototype.**

becomes

Todd refused the plan to build a new prototype.

or

Todd refused to build a new prototype.

Practice Sentence # 5

The lab took an analysis of the sample.

becomes

The lab analyzed the sample.

Practice Sentence # 6

The board arrived at a determination that the policy needed an overhaul.

becomes

The board determined that the policy needed an overhaul.

or

The board decided the policy needed an overhaul.

or

The board changed the policy.

Practice Sentence # 7

Please make a notation of your selection on the enclosed form.

becomes

Please note your selection on the enclosed form.

or

Please mark your choice on the enclosed form.

Practice Sentence # 8

After you have reviewed the enclosed material, please give consideration to becoming a sponsor for this program.

becomes

After you have reviewed the enclosed material, please consider becoming a sponsor for this program.

Practice Sentence # 9

Engineering made modifications to the galootin pin.

becomes

Engineering modified the galootin pin.

or

Engineering changed the galootin pin.

Practice Sentence # 10

I am appreciative of all your help.

becomes

I appreciate all your help.

In that activity you just completed, you might have noticed a certain detail. In the first nine sentences, you turned nouns back into strong verbs. In the tenth sentence, you changed an adjective, **appreciative**, back into the strong verb **appreciates**.

One more time - Why do people take perfectly good, strong verbs and weaken them by turning them into nouns or adjectives? You know – **100 Words - 10 Pages - 2 Blue Books. Big People Like Big Words - Big People Like Big Sentences.**

We started by discussing **Weak Verbs**.

We then moved on to the **Passive Voice**. Every time you use the **Passive Voice**, you must use a **Weak Verb** as part of that passive construction.

Then we moved on to **Nowhere Adverbs**. This word waster uses the word, *there*, followed by a **Weak Verb**.

Next came **Artificial Antecedents**. Using this construction forces you to use a **Weak Verb** or the **Passive Voice** with the pronoun, *it*.

We ended this section talking about **strong verbs that became nouns or**

adjectives. Each time you turn a good, strong verb into a noun or adjective, you must use a **Weak Verb** in the sentence.

Time Saving Bonus

If you completed each of the written exercises in this book, you recognize how much time the editing process takes. The good news is that you don't have to invest all that time each time you write. Let your computer perform the slave labor part of editing.

Let me explain. We discussed grammar checkers in the earlier part of the book. Your grammar checkers will find most instances where you have used the **Passive Voice**. They will also find many of the **verbs that became nouns or adjectives**. Some grammar checkers call them *difficult words* and some call them *wordy expressions*. Therefore, you don't have to spend time looking for them in your writing. Your computer will find them. You then must decide if or how you want to change them.

You can find **Nowhere Adverbs** and **Artificial Antecedents** just as easily. Your word processing program has a capability called **Edit**. Under the **Edit** menu, you should find a function called **Find** or **Find and Replace**. At this Find window, type in the word, *there*.

You know that a **Nowhere Adverb** is the word, *there,* and a **Weak Verb**. Your computer will find each instance in your writing where you have used the word, *there*. You can then decide if you have used a **Nowhere Adverb** and eliminate it to improve your writing.

Similarly, you know an **Artificial Antecedent** is the word *it* plus a **Weak Verb** or the **Passive Voice**. Again, under **Edit,** go to **Find or Find and Replace**, type in the word, *it*, and your computer will find each instance where you have used *it*. If you created an **Artificial Antecedent**, you can now change the sentence.

I have one caution for you. When you use the **Find** capability, be sure to set the search mode as **Whole** word. If you do not, your computer will stop each time it comes to the letters *i* and *t*. Thus, you might use the word *profit* and your computer will stop because it found the letters *i* and *t* in that word.

How To Get It Right When You Write

I also suggest you keep a list of other words, phrases and constructions that you can use the **Find** capability for. This list would include:

There	Insure
It	Myself/yourself
As	Per
Since	

Let me share with you why you should keep the above list near your computer.

You just found out why you should keep *there* and *it* on the list. You want *as* and *since* on your list because many people use these words incorrectly as a substitute for *because*.

I include the word "insure" on this list because many people confuse the words *insure, ensure* and *assure*.

Insure means to protect against loss.

Ensure means to guarantee certainty.

Assure means to fill with confidence.

Too many people use the word *insure*, when they mean *ensure*. Check your writing from time to time to see if you fall into this category.

Writers too often use *myself* and *yourself* when they should use *me* and *you*.

Consider the following sentences.

> *That project was completed by myself.*
>
> *They contacted Cathy and myself.*
>
> *The check was cashed by myself.*
>
> *Art and myself will handle all the arrangements.*
>
> *As a favor to myself, I took a two day vacation.*

Four of those sentences are incorrect. Do you know which four? If you said the first four, you are correct.

Here's why. To correctly use *myself* or *themselves*, the sentence must contain a noun or pronoun that *myself* or *themselves* refer to. Notice the first four sentences do not contain such references. The fifth sentence contains the pronoun *I*, which *myself* refers to.

The first four sentences should read:

> **The project was completed by me.**
>
> **They contacted Cathy and me.**
>
> **The check was cashed by me.**
>
> **Art and I will handle all the arrangements.**

The word *per* is on this list because people use this word incorrectly in the phrase, *per your request*. You will learn more about these errors in the next chapter.

For now, I ask you to remember them in your **Find** and **Replace** list.

As part of the **Time Saving Bonus**, let me offer you another tip. This is how I work. If it works for you, great.

After I create my document, I run it through my **Spell Checker**. When I am satisfied my spelling is correct, I print the document. Then, with a hard copy as a reference, I run my document through the **Grammar Checker**.

Rather than trying to use the grammar checker interactively, I choose to review what the grammar checker says about my writing and then highlight my mistakes on the hard copy. Then I go back and correct my original.

I do this because the hard copy allows me to see the whole document rather than a sentence in isolation the way grammar checkers work. I can see what I wrote before and after the error the grammar checker finds and decide if or how I want to change the sentence.

Also, this method creates an audit trail for me that documents what errors consistently show up in my writing. By reviewing the highlighted sentences, I can see what errors I need to spend time on correcting.

Remember that writing and editing are separate stages of writing. Don't try to edit your writing as you write. Write the way you speak. Then edit out these common errors. Don't do it while you're writing, or you will go nuts or get totally frustrated.

CHAPTER REVIEW

The following points highlight the more important topics discussed in this chapter. Scan them to see how many you can explain to someone else. If you cannot, I hope you invest the time to review them before moving on to the next section.

Avoid Weak Verbs

Am / Are / Is / Was / Were / Be / Been	Have / Has / Had	Make / Take / Give
	Do / Did / Done	

I *am* in need of help with my writing.

becomes

I *need* help with my writing.

Avoid Passive Voice

Here's how you spot the **Passive Voice**.

- The verb of the sentence contains a **Weak Verb** helping a strong verb.
- The subject of the sentence is not performing the action indicated by the verb.
- The person or thing performing the action becomes less important as the object of a preposition at the end of the sentence. Or, you may not even find the doer of the action mentioned in the sentence.

This sentence *was written* in the **Passive Voice**.

becomes

I *wrote* this sentence in the **Active Voice**.

Avoid Nowhere Adverbs

The word *there* followed by a **Weak Verb**.

> If you want to become a better writer, *there are* a few things you should avoid.

becomes

> If you want to become a better writer, you *should avoid* a few things.

Avoid Artificial Antecedents

The pronoun, *it,* without a logical antecedent followed by a **Weak Verb** or the **Passive Voice**.

> *It is* a lot of fun to get results from good writing.

becomes

> You will enjoy getting results from good writing.

or

> I enjoy getting results from my writing.

Again, say what you mean and mean what you say.

Avoid Turning Strong Verbs Into Nouns Or Adjectives

Watch out for words that end in *ion, tion, ation, al, ment, sis* or *ive*.

- *give a demonstration* means *demonstrate*
- *take a look at* becomes *look at* or *review*
- *make a recommendation* means *recommend*

Grammar checkers and the ***Edit*** *capability* of your computer will save you a tremendous amount of time in the editing stage.

"... the biggest problem in business writing today is the overuse of the passive voice."

Chapter Four
Construction Signs That Mean Rough Road Ahead

Now that we've discussed how the misuse of verbs can affect your writing, let's review other constructions that create longer sentences, confuse the readers and weaken your writing.

The following list describes constructions that you should avoid in writing.

Avoid "Dang" Modifiers

Remember these things when you were in school – Dangling Modifiers, Dangling Participles? They were called *dangling* because they dangled off the end of a sentence. They dangled, from either the beginning or the end of the sentence, not connected to the appropriate part of the sentence. For example:

> **Completely dissatisfied with the product, the salesman returned our money.**

According to that sentence, who was dissatisfied? That sentence says the salesman was dissatisfied. I believe the sentence should read:

> *Completely dissatisfied with the product, we asked the salesman to return our money.*

or

> *The salesman returned our money because we were completely dissatisfied with the product.*

Let's try another.

> **Shooting sparks into the air, the technician quickly turned off the motor.**

Do you get a mental picture here? According to this sentence, the technician is shooting the sparks. I don't think that was the intent of the sentence. It should probably read:

> *The technician quickly turned off the motor that was shooting sparks into the air.*

Again, you may have changed the sentence differently. That's great! That's the whole point of this book. When you write, you must clearly state what you mean in words that your reader will interpret the same way.

> **With an outstanding record of achievement, we bought Sam a drink and got his dog one too.**

According to this sentence, who had the outstanding record of achievement? It could have been Sam; it could have been us; it could have been Sam's dog. Technically, according to the sentence, we were the ones with the outstanding record. That may not have been the intent of the sentence.

I heard the next example on a flight to Nashville. As the flight attendant presented the pre-flight announcements, she said:

> **When turned on, the captain expects you to observe the "No Smoking" and "Fasten Seat Belt" signs.**

I had a problem with that statement. I did not know whether I was supposed to be looking at blinking lights, packing my nose with funny stuff or whether the crew started to party in the cockpit.

The next day, I left Nashville heading for Knoxville. The flight attendant on that flight announced:

> **We have open seating on this flight. We ask nonsmokers not to sit in the last four rows which are "Smoking."**

I wanted to get off that plane so fast!

Let me share one more bit of airline comedy.

As I was landing at the Pittsburgh International Airport, I heard the flight attendant, in a somewhat confusing way, offer passengers this piece of information.

> **If you are not familiar with the Pittsburgh airport, you will find a map of all of the gates on page 49 of our in-flight magazine.**

I **am** familiar with the Pittsburgh airport. Does that mean that if I look on page 49 I will **not** find a map?

Perhaps the airlines might consider saying:

Construction Signs That Mean Rough Road Ahead

> *If you are not familiar with the Pittsburgh airport, please check page 49 of our in-flight magazine for a map of the airport gates.*

Let's try a similar **Dang Modifier** in a business letter.

> **If you should have any questions or require any additional information, I may be reached at 1-800-555-5555.**

I guess that means if I don't have any questions, I have to dial another number to find this person.

What this confusing sentence should really say is:

> *If you have any questions or require any additional information, please call 1-800-555-5555.*

Let's check out one final example and move on.

> **Screaming wildly with pain, I put the burn victim in the ambulance.**

According to this sentence, the paramedic is doing the screaming. I'm sure many of you have heard the expression, ***Paint a picture with words.*** You can do that. But please, make sure the picture you paint is correct.

I hope this sentence meant:

> *The burn victim screamed wildly with pain as I helped him into the ambulance.*

To help you avoid **Dang Modifiers**, use your grammar checkers, read your writing out loud, use a twenty-four hour drawer, and then let your friends read your writing before you send it.

 **YOU NEED A PEN OR PENCIL NOW!**

Avoid Needless Words

On the next page you will find an activity that requires a pen or pencil. Until now, I have asked you to rewrite or edit individual sentences. Now

How To Get It Right When You Write

you get a chance to practice your editing skills on a memo. In the memo below, please draw a line through or put an (X) over all the **Needless Words** in the memo. When you are done, check out how I recommend editing the sample.

Needless Words

To:	Mononga Hela
From:	Al Agheny
Subject:	Overtime Abuses

The purpose of this memo is to provide information with respect to the subject of overtime abuses.

It has come to my attention that our labor cost allotment has more or less doubled this pay period. What is confusing is the fact that we are currently in or about the middle of our slow season.

We must herewith take a look at these types of excesses in the area of undue or unnecessary overtime as one of the most important focal issues at our next upcoming planning meeting. Overtime pay has exceeded the amount of $25,000, and we must not allow ourselves to procrastinate with regards to this matter of overtime.

You need not attempt to implement any changes until I have had the opportunity to present some clearly seen observations and I find myself in a position to make recommendations that, all things being equal, are fair and equitable to all.

Construction Signs That Mean Rough Road Ahead

Let's Compare Notes

In my seminars, about 25% of the participants wipe out the whole first sentence.

Some people eliminate **The purpose of**, some **is to**, some **with respect to** or **the subject of**. Technically, you don't need, nor do you want, the whole first sentence. This sentence tells you nothing more than you found in the **Subject Line**. It adds no power, no strength and no meaning.

Let's move to the second paragraph. I hope all of you wiped out, **It has come to my attention**. Did you remember this as an **Artificial Antecedent**? Great! Next, I hope you got rid of *more or less*.

Next, you should have wiped out, **What is confusing is the fact that**, **currently**, and **or about the**.

In the third paragraph, I hope you got rid of **herewith**. I never did understand that word. "Who are you herewith?" "Oh, I don't know."

Also, you could have drawn a line through *take a*. Have you ever noticed how people are always taking things?

> *I'd like to take this opportunity...*

> *I would like to take a moment to...*

This sample sentence allows you to attack it with your own style and purpose. You could have said:

> *We must look at excesses in overtime...*

or

> *We must look at unnecessary overtime...*

or

> *We must look at overtime...*

The phrase *as one of the most important focal issues* should read:

> *as the focal issue*.

A *focal issue* is the most important issue. That's why we refer to it as the *focal issue*. We focus on it.

Notice the phrase, ***next upcoming***. This is redundant. ***Next*** and ***upcoming*** mean the same thing.

In the next sentence, I eliminated ***the amount of,*** and I put a period after $25,000 and got rid of the rest of the sentence.

The last paragraph of the sample memo is absolutely dreadful. You don't need ***clearly seen***. Observations are things we see clearly.

I love ***I find myself in a position***. What is that position — Standing, sitting, lying, laying?

I like the phrase *find myself*. I never knew the person was lost.

Then you come to ***make recommendations*** rather than the good strong verb, ***recommend***.

How many of you put an (X) through the whole memo? You could have and maybe should have. Did you find a purpose for this memo? I didn't. Most of the participants in my seminars don't. If you put an (X) through the whole memo, congratulations.

Let's review a list of other **Needless Words** we see in writing all too regularly.

Sample Needless Words		
In many cases	In the area of	The fact that
Despite the fact that	Type of	At the present time
Needless to say	In order that	Meet with approval
In the amount of	In summation	In accordance with
At this point in time	That are designed to	As of this date
With respect to	In the event that	As a result of
In view of	In regard to	In conjunction with
For the purpose of	Prior to	Once all of the
Considering the fact that	I would like to	Due to the fact that

Construction Signs That Mean Rough Road Ahead

I'm going to review a selected few of these and give you some reasons why they are **Needless Words**.

Needless to say

This phrase has fascinated me for years. If something is "needless to say," why say it? I mention this, however, for a more specific reason. Suppose that, for whatever reason, you wanted to use that phrase. But, when you typed it, you typed, *needless to day*. Would your computer spell checker pick that up? Nope. It would go shooting right on by it. That's why I say, **Business Writing is a team sport**. Don't rely strictly on your spell checkers. Always give those important business documents to someone else to read before you send them.

In the amount of

Write me a check in the amount of one hundred dollars. No! Write me a check for one hundred dollars.

At this point in time

That phrase contains five words. What does that phrase mean? **NOW!** One simple, specific, powerful word with exact meaning. Why would normally rational, reasonable humans want to write five words when one would do? You know. **100 Words - 10 Pages - 2 Blue Books. Big People Like Big Words - Big People Like Big Sentences.**

That are designed to

Simply use *that*. For example:

> **I am sending you an affamit that is designed to reduce the wear on the motor.**

becomes

> ***I am sending you an affamit that will reduce wear on your motor.***

In the event that

Again, get real! Don't use four words for the beautiful word, *if.*

In regard to

Use *regarding*. That uses three syllables. The other way you force your readers to read four.

Prior to

Use *before*. Two syllables rather than three.

Due to the fact that

You already know two reasons **why** people use this phrase.

1. Fear of starting a sentence with *Because*.
2. **100 Words - 10 Pages - 2 Blue Books. Big People Like Big Words - Big People Like Big Sentences.**

Avoid Clichés

Sample Clichés	
Pressed into service	Smile on his face
Last but not least	Cool as a cucumber
Glutton for punishment	All in all
Light years ahead	Exercise my options
More than willing	More than happy
Keep in mind	Up to snuff
Grease the skids	By and large

The example list is only a partial list. I'm sure each of you could send me a list of 10 of your favorite clichés. If you did, I could compile them into an anthology of clichés.

Let's review just a few.

Pressed into service

What does that mean??? Some use this phrase to mean, *forced*. Unfortunately, most of the participants in my seminars are not sure what that phrase means. If you mean *forced*, use *forced*. If you mean *asked*, use *asked*.

Construction Signs That Mean Rough Road Ahead

Last but not least

I hope you're as tired of hearing and seeing this phrase as I am. Spend seven more seconds to become truly creative in your writing and infinitely more interesting.

Cool as a cucumber

Just how cool is a cucumber? Please allow me to tell you a story about this phrase.

I offer a writing workshop for highly technical people to show them how to get that great amount of information they keep locked in their heads released on paper so their work can be duplicated. I conducted a public seminar in Baltimore several years ago at the Omni Hotel. I will never forget this. The room was filled with 98 "Techies."

I came to the portion of the program where I talk about clichés, and I asked them the same question I asked you, "How many of you know how cool a cucumber is?"

I was not expecting an answer. However, one of the "Techies" sitting off to my right raised his hand.

I said, "Yes."

His chest puffed out and with confidence he said, "The inside temperature of a cucumber is five degrees lower than the ambient temperature of the room."

I didn't know what to say. Being a trained trainer, I turned to him and said, "Would you please repeat that for the rest of the audience?"

I needed time to think.

Again, his chest puffed out and with confidence he said, "The inside temperature of a cucumber is five degrees lower than the ambient temperature of the room."

This guy was a fabulous fund of fickle facts. So, I started telling this story in my workshops. A few weeks later, I told that story in Denver. A guy in the back of the room raised his hand and said, "That's not true."

I said, "What do you mean, that's not true?"

He said, "The inside temperature of a cucumber is five to eight degrees lower than the ambient temperature of the room."

Who cares!! Nobody knows; nobody cares.

That's the point. Nobody knows what these clichés mean or where they come from. So, why do people use them? All together now—**100 Words - 10 Pages - 2 Blue Books. Big People Like Big Words - Big People Like Big Sentences**.

More than willing

How could you be more than willing? Either you're willing or you're not.

More than happy

See above.

Up to snuff

What?!! Who is Snuff and why should we leave things up to him?

By and large

This one is my favorites. It has fascinated me for years. In that phrase, you find the word, *by*. ***By*** is a preposition. ***And*** is a conjunction. ***Large*** is an adjective.

A preposition requires an object. The object of a preposition is always a noun or pronoun. ***Large*** is an adjective!

A conjunction joins two like things. It does not join two *unlike* things. But here we have a conjunction joining a preposition and an adjective.

Enough about clichés. You get the idea.

Avoid Jargon

Every business, industry, government agency, organization and segment of society relies on its own set of words, phrases or acronyms to save time or space with internal communication. We call this form of internal verbal shortcuts **Jargon**. But that points out an important distinction — *internal communication*.

Construction Signs That Mean Rough Road Ahead

The problem is that too often, the habit of using **Jargon** extends beyond internal communication and becomes a tool you use with "outsiders." Those "outsiders" most often are employees or customers who don't know what the phrases mean. Remember, business people decide important issues based on what you write. If you use **Jargon** that your readers do not understand, you interrupt or delay their ability to make good decisions.

Do you remember the mystery of trying to understand computer terms and internet phrases? I think you get my point about **Jargon**.

Jargon tends to use more words than necessary to say something "outsiders" don't understand or care about. To show this, I will use my favorite examples from banking. I conduct a lot of in-house programs for banks and financial institutions, so I collect great examples from them.

I love when banks send me letters telling me I have an **"outstanding balance."** I write them back and say, "Thank you."

I don't have an **"outstanding balance."** I have a **balance**.

Then, when I visit the bank, I'm told to "see someone on the **platform**." So, I leave the bank and roam around to the back of the building to the loading dock looking for someone to answer my questions. Then, I send them a check and they write me back to let me know my loan is **"satisfied."** I am delighted to hear about the psychological health of my loan.

I think you get my point about **Jargon**.

Avoid Incorrect Grammar

I know you know you should avoid **Incorrect Grammar** in your business writing. I mention it here because many times, writers are not aware that some of the words or phrases they use are.

Consider these two phrases:

How To Get It Right When You Write

> **Between you and I**
>
> **For you and I**

I am amazed that people who are normally terrified of using the personal pronoun, *I* in business letters, will use it, but use it incorrectly. That should read:

> *Between you and me*
>
> *For you and me*

Also,

> **Where are you at?**
>
> **Where are you going to?**

All you have to say or write is:

> *Where are you?*
>
> *Where are you going?*

Avoid Localisms

I call the next writing error **Localism** because in my workshops I have a tough time pronouncing the word, "colloquialism." I also call them that because they tend to show up in local areas. Let me show you what I mean.

I'm not originally from Pittsburgh. I've lived here now for twenty years. During my first week in Pittsburgh, the kid next door came over and said to me, "Hey, your car needs washed."

Actually, what he said was, "your car needs warrshed."

I thought I had landed on another planet. I had never heard that expression anywhere.

Most of you realize he should have said, "Hey, your car needs *to be* washed." Or, "Your car needs washing." I don't know why, the people in Pittsburgh leave off the *to be* parts in their sentences, both in speech and writing.

They say and write things like:

Construction Signs That Mean Rough Road Ahead

That hole needs dug.

My check needs cashed.

Some questions need answered.

I guess if Shakespeare were born in Pittsburgh, Hamlet's famous line, "To be or not to be. That is the question." would become, "Or not."

Grammatically speaking, the above sentences should read:

That hole needs to be dug.

My check needs to be cashed.

Some questions need to be answered.

In New Orleans, the locals say, "Did you make groceries?" Or, they might ask, "Did you save the dishes?" In the first question, they mean, did you go to the store, buy groceries, come home, and put them away?

The second question means, did you wash the dishes and put them away?

In certain parts of New York state the locals say, "Give me a couple three reasons." How many do they want, two, three, five, six?

My point here is this. In the **Helpful Hints** section, you learned to find some friends to help improve your writing. I recommend you find some **friends who are not from your local area**. They will spot localisms quickly and easily.

If a person from Pittsburgh wrote a letter to a customer in Chicago and said, "Your account needs settled," can you imagine what the Chicago native would think?

When I lived in Massachusetts, I was in a Sears store at the Auburn Mall in Worcester. A guy walked up to me and asked me if I could tell him where he could find the "bubbler."

A big smile came to my face that conveniently covered my embarrassment and confusion. I had no idea what the man was asking me. And, I told him so.

I asked him, "What is a bubbler?" "Where do you keep it?" "What do you feed it?" He must have thought I was totally stupid so he told me a "bubbler" was a water fountain or, as some call it, a drinking fountain.

How To Get It Right When You Write

The only place I have ever heard a water fountain referred to as a "bubbler" was in New England and a narrow band of geography between Minnesota and Wisconsin.

To avoid **Localisms**, find some friends who are not from your local area.

Avoid Foreign Phrases

The following is a partial list.

Sample Foreign Phrases		
Voila	Ergo	Ipso facto
Coup de grace	Per se	Vis a vis
Caveat	In lieu of	Faux pas

Different people from different parts of the country or, with different backgrounds or education, use different **Foreign Phrases** in their writing. My point again is to show that most people use foreign phrases to impress people. **Foreign Phrases** do not impress me; they depress me. I don't know what these phrases mean. Many times your readers don't either.

The other reason you should avoid **Foreign Phrases** is that a lot of people feel the way I do. I take informal polls in my workshops and seminars. Many of the participants don't know what these phrases mean. And, these participants represent typical business writing **audiences**.

Even worse than the readers not knowing what these phrases mean, many of the people that include them in their writing don't know the correct meanings. Two stories will explain what I mean.

The first involves the French word, ***voila***. I conducted a workshop in Boston about nine years ago in which I talked about that word. I asked the participants to tell me what the phrase meant. I heard at least six different answers. At the lunch break, one of the participants thanked me for talking about the word, ***voila***.

She said she had only heard it two times in her life and that this workshop was the second time. She told me that the only other time she had heard the word was when she was in high school. At that time, the school board brought in a magician to perform. The magician reached into a black silk hat, pulled out a white rabbit by its ears and said, ***"Voila."***

The woman told me she thought that was the rabbit's name. That's how these foreign phrases affect people.

In my workshops, I ask people to explain the phrase ***"coup de grace."*** Some tell me it means, "a glorious ending," a "grand finale," a "final touch."

Do you know what a *coup de grace* really is? It's a shot to the head of a person who has been executed. It's a mercy killing to make sure the person is dead. A shot to the head, a stab to the heart. Now that's a "final touch!"

Here's another dandy, **caveat**. Simply put, a **caveat** is a warning. Be real. You do not see a message on a cigarette pack that says, ***Caveat. Smoking may be harmful to your health***.

Again, the point jumps out. Write to express, not impress. Avoid words and phrases that add length but no strength and can confuse your audience.

Please allow me one final reason why you should avoid using **foreign phrases**.

After the tragic high school shooting in Littleton, Colorado in 1999, a reporter started his column with the following sentence, ***In lieu of the Colorado tragedy... asked several teens whether something similar could occur at their high school.***

The phrase *in lieu of* means *instead of*. I guess even though the phrase was incorrect, it sounded impressive to the reporter.

Avoid Redundancy

Please review the sample list of **Redundant** phrases and the words you can use to replace them. Notice, I said *sample* list. This list is not a complete list. I'm not sure a complete list exists. This list represents the most commonly used phrases I see in the writing samples I work with. Your list might include other examples. After the list, I have included a discussion that explains **why** these phrases are **Redundant**.

How To Get It Right When You Write

Sample Redundancies	
One of the best	Continue to occur
Prior experience	Future prospects
True fact	Free of charge
Very unique	Basic fundamentals
Root causes	End result
Repeat again	Close proximity
Past history	Prior record
Exact same	Xerox copies

One of the best

You can only have one ***best***. If you want to compare someone or something, you must use the word, ***better***.

> *He is one of the better swimmers in the world.*

> *This is one of the better business writing books on the market.*

I can't say ***the best*** because I would somehow have to prove that to the Truth in Advertising Police.

I believe this phrase, ***one of the best*** was coined by an advertising person. I don't think a car company would place an ad on television that said, "We have one of the better cars in the world." Again, the Truth in Advertising Police would hunt them down. So, this marketing wizard used literary license to create, ***one of the best***.

Prior experience

All experience **is** prior. When did you get your experience? Prior to applying for a job.

True fact

Do we have "false facts?"

Free of charge

All you need to say is, *free*.

Free gift

Again, all you need to say is, *gift*. When did we start paying for gifts?

For example, consider these two sentences.

All guests will receive a free gift.

All guests will receive a gift.

Very unique

Also avoid qualifiers such as:

More unique

Most unique

Unique means *one of a kind*. Therefore, you cannot compare people or things in terms of their uniqueness. You can't say, "That lamp is most unique." That lamp is **unique**.

Close proximity

As opposed to *far proximity*?

Prior record

That criminal does not have a "prior" record; he has a "record."

Why do people use such redundant phrases?

1. **We are so accustomed to hearing them and seeing them in print.**
2. **100 Words - 10 Pages - 2 Blue Books. Big People Like Big Words - Big People Like Big Sentences.**

Avoid Polysyllabic Substitutions

Please don't panic. No, I am not trying to impress you or confuse you.

I use the phrase **Polysyllabic Substitutions** as an example of a **Polysyllabic Substitution**.

Let me explain **why** I used that phrase. The word *polysyllabic* means *having more than two syllables*. A **Polysyllabic Substitution**, then, means substituting a word that has *more* than two syllables for a word that has *less* than two.

Am I telling you to never use words that contain more than two syllables? No, of course not. I am saying that in business writing, you should use words that most people recognize and understand.

I used the words ***Artificial Antecedent*** to describe the ***it thing***. I used that phrase, as I suggested, for shock value. However, the word ***artificial*** is a word I believe most people are familiar with. It is a word most people know and understand.

Please review the list of words that follow this paragraph. I used those words in the two paragraphs above. Each word in the list contains more than two syllables:

Syllables	Business	Recognize	Suggested
However	Artificial	Familiar	Understand
Paragraphs	Following		

Although those words had more than two syllables, you understood them.

The point here is simple. In your business writing, rely more on shorter words that your readers will understand quickly and easily. Even if they do understand the longer word, you save time and space using the shorter words and the readers save time reading and understanding your meaning.

Indeed, sometimes even short words cause problems for some readers. Consider the word, ***nee.*** This is a very short word! However, many people do not know what it means. The dictionaries tell us the word means ***born***. The word ***nee*** appears after a married woman's name to indicate her maiden name. For example, Mary Jones, nee Smith, means Mary's maiden name was Smith.

Again, the message is simple. Use words to express a thought your readers can grasp easily and quickly. Don't use words to fill pages or sound educated.

Construction Signs That Mean Rough Road Ahead

Another reason you should avoid some of these words is that many people use the words and do not understand what the real meanings of the words are.

Below, you will find a sample list of **Polysyllabic Substitutions**. After the list, you will find a brief discussion of **why** you should eliminate specific **Polysyllabic Substitutions**. If you do not know a one or two syllable word to replace the words in this list, perhaps your readers might not know what the word means.

Sample Polysyllabic Substitutions		
Utilize	Commence	Scrutinize
Demonstrate	Exemplify	Forwarded
Cognizant	Subsequent	Finalize
Interrogate	Institute	Prioritize
Paradigm	Approximately	Reiterate
Initiate	Irregardless	Execute
Modify	Altercation	Detrimental
Eradication	Ascertain	Articulate
Terminate	Optimum	Affluent
Consequence	Transpire	Reimburse
Recapitulation	Endeavor	Parameters
Disseminate	Facilitate	Implement
Remuneration	Heretofore	Purchase
Validate	Incarcerate	Methodology
Ameliorate	Effectuate	Conundrum
Shibboleth	Expeditious	Proficiency

Let's talk about some of these.

Utilize

This may be the dumbest word in the English language.

First, *utilize* is a made up word. Watch out for any word that ends in *ize*. That normally means it's made up to sound impressive and fill pages.

Second, at least half of the times when I hear or read the word, the people using the word are using it incorrectly or they are using the wrong word. The words *use* and ***utilize*** do not mean the same thing. Let me put it to you this way.

You can use the word ***utilize*** from now until the day you die and be wrong at least 50% of the time. You can use the word, ***use*** and never be wrong.

Which odds do you like? If you don't believe me, look up both words in the dictionary. "Ah," you say to me. "I don't have time to look them up." Alas, you get my meaning. Your readers don't have time, nor do they want to look up fancy words in the dictionary. Use the familiar, shorter versions. You will save time writing, typing or saying them. Your readers will save time because they don't have to stop to figure out what you mean or how you are using the word.

Simply drop the word ***utilize*** from your vocabulary and you will always be correct.

Demonstrate

This word contains three syllables. First, check out how many different interpretations you can get for that word.

Describe	Display
Explain	Reveal
Relate	Show
Prove	Teach

Five of those words contain two syllables and three contain only one syllable. We're talking clear, simple, easy to read, easy to understand and easy to remember. That's what good writing is all about.

Reiterate

I'm amazed at how many people talk about ***reiterating*** but few of them ever ***iterate***.

The word ***iterate*** means ***to utter again or repeatedly***. So if you reiterate, you're a babbling idiot.

Construction Signs That Mean Rough Road Ahead

Conundrum

This word means *a riddle, the answer to which involves a pun or a play on words*. The confusion sets in when writers use this to mean a mystery, or a problem that is difficult to understand or solve. This interpretation uses only half of the real meaning of the word. More importantly, it can confuse the readers and add length but no strength to the document.

Commence

I know. This word only contains two syllables. But I just don't like this word. What's wrong with *start* or *begin*?

Every time I hear or see this word I think of the old TV show **The Beverly Hillbillies**. Jed Clampett, Jethro, Ellie Mae, and Granny *commenced* to do everything!

On one show, Granny announced that Jethro was *commencing to begin building a root cellar*.

Transpire

People use this word to mean *to occur, happen or take place*. Actually, the dictionary warns us that those interpretations are considered incorrect or vulgar.

Prioritize

Prioritize maybe the second dumbest word in the English language. The reason is that it is not a word.

At least, most good dictionaries do not recognize it as a word. The word, *prioritize* did not appear in a dictionary until the year 1966. It was not accepted by most dictionaries until 1987. And you still won't find it in all dictionaries.

Some of you may have unknowingly proved this to yourselves. Participants in my workshops tell me they used the word in their writing and their spell checkers stopped and said, "word not found." Naturally, being resourceful people, they "added" it to their word processor's dictionary.

When *prioritize* first appeared in the dictionary in 1966, it was followed by the designation, (Coll), which means "colloquial." That means it is not a real word. But so many people use it, the dictionary publishers felt obliged to include it for those curious about its derivation.

If you look up the word, *"ain't"* in the dictionary, you also find the designation, (Coll). That means the words *prioritize* and *ain't* come from the same family. However, in this democratic republic we live in, where money, power, education, and status somehow prevail, you will see something interesting happening in a couple of years.

The word *ain't* will never lose its (Coll) designation. But the word *prioritize*, used by the people with the money, power, education, and status will forever leave the (Coll) designation behind. They will somehow conveniently bury its questionable lineage.

Oh! Yes, the word *prioritize* means *rank*.

I will rank these tasks in the order I intend to perform them.

not

I will prioritize the tasks in the order I intend to perform them.

Implement

This is a fancy word business people throw around to make their projects sound important and impressive.

The problem with using this word is that your readers interpret the word too many ways for you to leave your meaning to chance. In my workshops, participants tell me this word means, *do, complete, start, use,* or *put into action*. Among other things, the dictionary tell us it means *to satisfy a condition*.

I prefer to use one of those words or phrases to clearly state my idea.

Again, using shorter, familiar words will improve the chances that communication will take place clearly and correctly.

Subsequent

Never ever, ever, ever use this word or its other forms, **subsequently** or **subsequent to**, in business writing. I'm a **whys guy**. Let me tell you **why**.

Half the people in the world think that word means *before*; the other half think it means *after*. A third half thinks it means *later*. I don't care what it means! Think about this – *before* – *after* – *later,* three beautiful, short, specific, powerful words. Be kind to your readers. Don't allow them to spin off into an intense brain search to try to decide if you mean *before, after* or *later*.

Avoid A Preponderance of Prepositional Phrases

Please don't panic. Again, I use this horrible phrase as an example of the writing error it portrays.

When we talked about **Weak Verbs**, we talked about the effect of prepositional phrases on the length of sentences. A **Preponderance of Prepositional Phrases** will:

1. Add length but not necessarily strength to the sentence.
2. Confuse readers because they must determine which of the nouns in the sentence truly serves as the subject.
3. Force one page letters to become two pages.

For example:

Men of medicine generally manifest a predilection for an apparatus known in their esoteric nomenclature as a sphygmomanometer for the purpose of determining the systolic and diastolic parameters of their clientele in an effort to ascertain their degree of wellness.

This sounds impressive. All this really means is:

Doctors use an instrument to test your blood pressure.

If you see your role as educator to the world, you could become more informative and write:

Doctors use an instrument called a sphygmomanometer to test your blood pressure.

How To Get It Right When You Write

Avoid Weighted, Unnatural Language

The five examples below show what I mean by **Weighted, Unnatural Language**.

> **The contract stipulated exacting specifications for the installation of eight vertical access devices.**

I don't think people think this way, and I don't think people talk this way. The question becomes, "Why do people write this way?" Go ahead, say it to yourselves.

I love discussing this sentence in my workshops. The participants offer so many interesting interpretations. I get:

> *The contract called for eight doors.*

> *The contract called for eight windows.*

> *The contract called for eight ladders.*

> *The contract called for eight ropes.*

I once got:

> *The contract called for eight filing cabinets.*

The original intent of that sentence was:

> *The contract called for eight elevators.*

Let's try the second example.

> **The following are some of the problems which were instrumental in contributing to the dissolution of the program.**

I hope you would be conversational and real and write:

> *The following problems prompted us to cancel the program.*

or

> *The following problems caused us to cancel the program.*

or

> *We canceled the program because...*

Construction Signs That Mean Rough Road Ahead

or

I canceled the program because...

The third example is a short sentence. However, check out the fifty dollar words that make this a masterpiece of muddled malarkey.

We have not commenced to evolve a solution to your unfortunate situation.

Be real! People don't think that way; people don't talk that way.

A Golden Oldie song title should help you with this sentence - *"Tell It Like It Is."*

We need more time to solve your problem.

or,

We haven't started working on your... because...

I read the next example in a newspaper.

A seat on the school board also allows them more easily to obfuscate any complicity the teachers union may have in declining educational standards.

What!!!

The final example also requires no comment. It is a real example written by a real person.

The not inconsiderable dangers inherent in the possibility of expanding the concept to the point where it becomes meaningless seems to us to be compensated by the possibility of increasing the effectiveness of the program.

Next!!!

Avoid Weak Openings and Weak Closings

Below, you will find a partial list of **Weak Openings** and **Weak Closings**. At the end of the list, I will share with you **why** these are poor ways to start or end a business document.

I'm sure you're going to see one or two of your favorites in this list. Please read the reasons **why** you should avoid them and how changing them might improve your writing.

Sample Weak Openings and Weak Closings	
Please be advised	As you are aware
Under separate cover	Attached herewith
The above mentioned	If at all possible
We note the inclusion of	The aforementioned
We regret to inform you	Per your request
Thanking you in advance	It is our intention
Currently we are developing	Attached please find
Efforts have been taken to	It is our understanding
Enclosed please find	Under the circumstances
According to our records	Don't hesitate to call
Your request has been received	Feel free to call
Pursuant to your request	In light of recent

Let's explore *why* these are weak openings and weak closings by using a few examples.

Enclosed please find

To explain why this is a weak opening, we need to return to our story about the four kinds of sentences. In fifth and sixth grade, you learned about Declarative, Interrogative, Exclamatory, and Imperative sentences. You also learned that an Imperative sentence is a command, a demand, or an order.

When you begin a letter with, **Enclosed please find**, you are using an imperative sentence. That means you are commanding, demanding, or ordering your readers to perform an action. Rather than commanding, demanding, or ordering your readers, I suggest you use a simple, Declarative sentence that starts, **I have enclosed**.

Why do people use **Enclosed please find**? The answer is simple. They are terrified of starting a sentence with *I*. They are terrified of using personal pronouns in business documents. **Why** does this fear exist? Participants tell me that they were told, "Never start a sentence with *I*

Construction Signs That Mean Rough Road Ahead

because it would sound like they were bragging."

When you say **Enclosed please find**, the reader has responsibility for the action. When you use **I have enclosed**, you assume responsibility. You have now taken the heat off of the reader and have become more **personal**.

Please be advised

When you use this phrase you are saying to the reader, "Sit up and pay attention, dummy, I've got something important to tell you." Again, notice you are using an imperative sentence.

Let me show you the subtle differences in approach, and you decide which would work better for you.

Please be advised we will be closed Monday.

or

We will be closed Monday.

Notice that in the second example, you used three less words and changed the sentence from imperative to declarative.

I know! You want to make this stand out. You want the readers to know that this piece of information is important. When manual typewriters served as the highest form of office technology, the phrase, **Please be advised**, might have caught readers' attention. Manual, and even electric typewriters, allowed little graphic capability.

Today, using your computers and modern printers, you can:

> **Bold Information**
> *Use italics*
> • Use Bullets
> *Change the font*
> Change the font size
> Use text boxes, borders or graphics
> Use *D*rop cap from your format menu
> Center the information
> *Use combinations of the above*

Warning:

<u>DO NOT UNDERLINE OR USE ALL CAPS (UPPER CASE)</u>

Underlining makes reading more difficult for your eyes and mind. If you don't believe me, compare what I created in the text box versus the example I underlined and decide for yourself.

Studies show that reading a combination of upper case and lower case letters is easier and faster to read than all upper case.

The above mentioned

and

The aforementioned

Both of these phrases can become a source of confusion for some readers. The following sample memo will show how these words or phrases might be interpreted.

To: M. Phatic

From: D. Termined

Subject: P.O. Number 12345

Date: August 8, 1996

We have received your inquiry about the above mentioned. Our customer service department will research your order.

The aforementioned will then become part of our extended care customer service system.

You will be contacted when the above mentioned becomes a reality.

Thank you.

Construction Signs That Mean Rough Road Ahead

Let me use this sample memo to explain why you should not use **the above mentioned** or **the aforementioned**. Technically speaking, when you use those phrases, they refer to the contents of the subject line. In this instance, every time we used those phrases, it referred to P.O. Number 12345.

The problem comes about for those readers who do not understand or know this rule. Thus, in the second paragraph, readers may wonder whether the phrase **the aforementioned** refers to the P.O. itself, the customer service department, or the status of the order. The question becomes, what will become "part of the extended customer service care system?"

In the third paragraph, again, the reader may wonder what will become "a reality." Will it be the order, the customer service department or the extended care customer service system?

All of this confusion comes about because of a deeply seated fear of using the same word or phrase more than once in a sentence or paragraph.

I recommend you change the memo to read:

To: M. Phatic

From: D. Termined

Subject: P.O. Number 12345

Date: August 8, 1996

We have received your inquiry about **P.O. Number 12345**. Our customer service department will research your order to see which items are on back order.

Your inquiry and a complete response will then become part of our extended care customer service system that ensures your complete satisfaction.

We will call you within 24 hours to let you know when we will ship the remainder of your order and by which carrier.

Thank you.

Notice we changed this letter to become more specific, more personal, and easier to read and understand. Indeed, we did make the letter longer. This becomes another example of where sometimes you must sacrifice your conciseness to get the results you want. In this instance, I hope the results mean a satisfied customer.

The first sample memo displayed a legalistic, impersonal tone that sounded like an obligatory response.

We regret to inform you

This opening is weak because it presents a negative tone and a poor approach to the subject and the reader. The next section of this book will discuss the benefits of presenting a positive tone in your writing.

For now, ask yourself whether the person or people writing the letter really *regret to inform you*.

As you are aware

I recommend you do not use this phrase because of the multiple messages this phrase sometimes communicates. The problem with this phrase is that some people might feel embarrassed, intimidated, or threatened. Notice, I said some people.

You may feel this phrase is a useful transitional phrase or a helpful reminder to the reader. Workshop participants offer other interpretations. Some readers interpret that phrase to mean, "You had better be aware." This comes across as threatening and intimidating. I understand not everyone feels that way about this phrase.

But, enough participants in my workshops have voiced those feelings for me to include it in this book.

Feel free to call

I know! You're mad at me for telling you to get rid of one of your favorite expressions. Let me share the *why* with you. To do that, let me use a closing that I frequently see in business writing.

Construction Signs That Mean Rough Road Ahead

 **YOU NEED A PEN OR PENCIL NOW!**

If you have any questions, please feel free to call.

With your pen or pencil, cross out the words,"feel free to." You now have:

If you have any questions, please call.

Are you really serious about having people call you? If you are, you would probably write:

If you have any questions, please call me.

Your business writing has just become more specific, personal, and shorter. You used two less words and this helps you get to your goal of averaging 18 words per sentence.

Two more reasons for changing this sentence relate to the **Subject-Verb- Relationship** and the results you want to achieve.

In the original example, the verb of the sentence is *feel*. In the suggested version, the verb becomes *call*. What action do you expect them to perform? Do you want them to *feel* or do you want them to *call*?

Please don't hesitate to call

Many people end their messages with the following sentence.

 **YOU NEED A PEN OR PENCIL NOW!**

If you have any questions, please don't hesitate to call.

With your pen or pencil, cross out **don't hesitate to**. Look what you have now done.

How To Get It Right When You Write

1. You used three less words.
2. You have shifted from the negative tone to a positive tone.
3. You have eliminated a double negative.
4. You have used the correct **Subject - Verb - Relationship** to get the results you're looking for.

If you want them to call, say so. I actually hear from my workshop participants that they will use the phrase **don't hesitate to call** to make sure people don't call them. That phrase becomes a form of reverse psychology. Let me explain what I mean by that.

If you've ever flown on a plane, you know exactly how reverse psychology works. Before the plane can take off, the flight attendants recite the pre-flight announcements. They generally concluded their announcements with," If we can be of any further assistance to you, **please don't hesitate to call** on any of us."

What are they telling you? "Sit down, shut up, buckle up, and don't bother us. We are trying to get the plane in the air."

In a previous chapter, I bragged about my daughter's twins. Let me share with you how early reverse psychology becomes a part of us.

One night, Marylou and I were at Chris's house when she was giving the twins a bath. At the time, the twins were only 18 months old. An important part of the bathing ritual is the accumulation of floatable distractions. Among these distractions, Chris bought plastic alphabet letters that stick to a wall, the tub, or a child when they (the letters or the kids) are wet.

Alexandra became extremely delighted in tossing these wet letters out of the tub. Mommy said, "Alexandra don't throw the letters out of the tub." At which, Alexandra increased the speed and number of letters that left the tub.

Grammy came up with a great idea. "Alexandra, why don't you put all those letters in your little pail?" Again, the volume and speed of projectiles increased.

Construction Signs That Mean Rough Road Ahead

Then Grampy in a hushed, secretive, personal tone, huddled over Alexandra and whispered, "Alexandra, listen. Don't put any of those letters into that pail."

You guessed it. Alexandra immediately started filling the pail with the letters.

If you really want your customers to call you with questions, let your written words prove that. Rather than:

If you have any questions, please don't hesitate to call.

write

If you have any questions, please call me.

If you are really serious you would write:

If you have any questions, please call at 1-800-555-1234, extension 2929.

Per your request

or

Pursuant to your request

To understand why you should not use these two phrases, you need only remember Mr. Iacocca's words. "If you don't talk that way, don't write that way." In conversations, most people do not use the phrase, **per your request**. Most people would say, *"As you requested."*

Check out what happens when you do this. In the phrase *per your request*, **per** is a preposition, **your** is an adjective, **request** is a noun used as the object of the preposition.

When you use the phrase, *as you requested*, **you** becomes a subject; **requested** becomes a verb. What is the key to good writing? The **Subject – Verb – Relationship**.

In the phrase, *per your request*, decide which is the most important word. Most workshop participants offer **request** as the most important word.

In the phrase, *as you requested*, decide the most important word. Most workshop participants select **you**. Notice again, how the suggested version becomes more personal.

If you prefer another source to verify what I have said above, please check the Gregg Reference Manual, Section 11 – Usage, under the word **per** where they state:

> **"NOTE: Do not use *per* in the sense of according to or in accordance with. We are sending you samples *as you requested*. (NOT: per your request.)"**

Let me give you another reason why you should eliminate these weak openings and weak closings.

How many of you reading this book are named, ***Occupant***? I can see quite a few of you saying, "Boy, he really knows me." Those of you who are not named ***Occupant*** go by another name, ***Resident***. Some of you have a first name, ***Current***.

Every time you use these weak openings and closings, you telegraph to your readers: Dear Occupant; Dear Resident.

And, you send a very clear message to your readers. "Hey, I'm an important person. I'm a busy person. I don't have time to write you a personal note. So, I'm going to use these phrases (I don't have a clue what they mean or where they came from) but I have to get this stupid thing written and off my desk." You are telling the readers, "I don't care about you. I care about me."

Remember, communication means ***caring and sharing.***

When you use these phrases, another big red flag waves in front of your readers. That red flag has the words "junk mail" prominently displayed on it. I am willing to bet all of you can spot junk mail in your mail box from three blocks away. You don't like junk mail; you know what results junk mail gets.

Please understand that I am not telling you not to invite people to call. I am saying that rather than using worn out, empty phrases, you can get better results with a fresh personal approach.

Construction Signs That Mean Rough Road Ahead

Avoid The Gender Syndrome

The **Gender Syndrome** refers to the use of sexist terms in business writing. For example, consider the following three sentences.

> **The creative writer does not wait for chance to bring him inspiration; he develops his own.**
>
> **Every supervisor must sign the time cards of his workers.**
>
> **Each traveler carried his own luggage to the plane.**

Each of these sentences refers to a masculine pronoun, ***him***, ***he*** or ***his***.

The first sentence implies only men know how to write and we can only find one of them. The second sentence implies only men can become managers. The third limits air travel to men.

Let me show you how to change these sentences quickly and easily to become grammatically and politically correct.

Earlier, you learned about **Artificial Antecedents**. Antecedents again will play an important role in correcting these sentences. The **Gender Syndrome** comes about by the incorrect use of pronouns, in this instance, masculine pronouns that exclude women.

The first step to correct the **Gender Syndrome** involves finding the bothersome pronouns. The first example included three bothersome pronouns — ***him, he*** and ***his***. The next step requires you to identify the antecedents of those pronouns. In the sample sentence, the antecedent of all three pronouns is the same — ***writer***. The third step simply involves changing the antecedent from singular to a plural designation. This means you must change the pronouns to become plural.

That would change the sentence to read:

> *Creative writers do not wait for chance to bring them inspiration; they develop their own.*

Notice also that when you pluralize the subject of the sentence, ***writers***, you must change the verb to read correctly. You wouldn't say:

> *Creative writers does not wait for chance...*

You change the verb from *does* to *do*.

The second example should read:

All supervisors must sign the time cards of their workers.

Here again, you found the bothersome pronoun, *his*; you found the antecedent, *supervisor*; you pluralized *supervisor*, and you pluralized *his* to *their*.

The third example should read:

All travelers carried their luggage to the plane.

Notice in that sentence, you also eliminated the word *own*. The pronoun, *their*, shows that ownership.

Avoid Negative Tone

Tell your readers what you can or will do for them, not what you can't or won't do. Tell your readers what they can or should do, not what they can't do.

Simply put, you will get better results with a positive tone.

Let me use an example to show you how this tone thing works. Pretend you get home from work to find an important looking letter in your mail box. You open the letter and the first sentence starts, "We regret to inform you..."

After those first four words, how do you feel? Positive words tend to produce more positive results than negative words.

Let me show you how to change negative statements into positive ones.

Please don't hesitate to call.

We've already talked about this one.

Please call.

Please call me.

Please call me at ...

Construction Signs That Mean Rough Road Ahead

Next example:

> **I won't be in my office until June 3rd.**
>
> becomes
>
> *I will be in my office June 3rd.*
>
> or
>
> *Call me after June 3rd.*
>
> or
>
> *I will send that information to you when I return to my office on June 3rd.*

Next example:

> **The new product line can't be sold until the third quarter.**
>
> becomes
>
> *The new product line will be available starting the third quarter.*
>
> or
>
> *We will begin shipping the new product line in the third quarter.*
>
> or
>
> *You will receive the new product line early in the third quarter.*
>
> or
>
> *You will receive the new product line the first week of September.*

Notice in the last sentence, we became more specific. Rather than saying, "the third quarter," we used, "September." If you write your document in the early part of the year and use a phrase like, "the third quarter," your readers might get the impression that is a long way off. Being specific and telling them a month gives them a better feeling because of the specific information.

> **We have no more rooms on the first floor.**

Again, this sentence contains a negative tone. The sentence takes on a positive tone by saying:

All our first floor rooms are occupied.

The next example may be a statement of truth. The tone, however, might leave the reader a little cold.

I don't have time to review your proposal now.

This becomes a kinder, gentler, more reader-focused sentence when you say:

I will review your proposal this afternoon when I can give it my undivided attention.

Yes, you used more words. But, I believe the results you get with this approach will prove worthy of your investment.

Next,

We don't sell used equipment.

Proudly state what you do sell.

We sell only new equipment.

The next example uses the negative tone and hints at the words your readers focus on.

Our meeting shouldn't last more than two hours.

Stated positively, the sentence reads:

Our meeting will last less than two hours.

When you read the first example, your mind focuses on the word, ***more***, not the negative, ***shouldn't***. So your readers get the impression that the meeting **will** last ***more*** than two hours.

The better word for your readers to focus on is ***less***. Your readers take a more positive attitude toward the meeting because it would take less of their time.

I offer the final example to show you where you might want to stress the negative. Also, the example shows the need to become clear and concise. That means getting to the message quickly and clearly.

Do not use this water for drinking purposes.

Construction Signs That Mean Rough Road Ahead

That sentence was on a sign I once saw. I would prefer this sign to read:

Don't drink this water!

Avoid Abstract and Non-specific Terms

Abstract and **Non-specific Terms** are those words or phrases that you cannot see, taste, touch, smell, hear or count. For example,

The function will feature participatory activities.

This sentence does not tell you what the *function* is or what the *participatory activities* are. Be specific; be graphic. Write:

The company picnic will feature a softball game and an egg-throwing contest.

Let's try another.

Brian is an *excellent* student.

My definition of an excellent student and my son's don't even come close. My definition of an excellent student is an A plus student. For my son, C is an excellent grade. "But dad, I work two jobs, I play in the band, and I have to go to all those parties." I guess in those situations, C is an excellent grade.

How about:

He amassed a *fortune* extracting *subterranean substances*.

A fortune to me and, maybe to you, versus a fortune to Bill Gates or Donald Trump or Ross Perot, do not mean the same thing. We're not even in their league. Be specific:

He became a gazillionaire mining gold.

Here's another:

Weather conditions prohibited our *planned agenda*.

Now, you really know a lot. This sentence tells you nothing.

Snow canceled our pool party.

One final example:

It seems the *device* is *malfunctioning*.

The question becomes, what is the device and how is it malfunctioning?

The air conditioner is spitting flames.

Now your readers get the picture.

Avoid Lack of Parallelism

Earlier, one of the Helpful Hints was, "**Read Your Writing Out Loud.**" Read the sample sentence out loud and you will understand what that Helpful Hint meant. Go ahead, no one's around. Read it out loud.

I like hunting, fishing and to go swimming.

Did that hurt your ears? Something *sounded* wrong. Even though you may not be able to recite the grammar rule that applies here, you know something is wrong. The sample sentence contains an example of lack of parallelism. Without getting technical, you can tell me that the phrase *to go swimming* doesn't fit with the words, *hunting* and *fishing*. True. That construction is not parallel. That sentence should read:

I like hunting, fishing and swimming.

Read the next one out loud. Go ahead; you're on a roll.

He is friendly, kind, thrifty, brave, and goes to church.

Again, you know something sounds funny. The verb phrase, "Goes to church," does not fit with the adjectives, *friendly*, *kind*, *thrifty*, and *brave*.

It should read:

He is friendly, kind, thrifty, brave, and reverent.

or

He is friendly, kind, thrifty, brave, and church-going.

The next example is simply poor grammar.

Him and I are headed for the shore.

Construction Signs That Mean Rough Road Ahead

I seriously doubt that a person that would write or say that sentence would write or say, "Him is headed for the shore." I'm sure that person would say, "He is headed for the shore." Just because you added the personal pronoun "I" to the sentence is no reason to change the first one. The sentence becomes parallel when you write:

He and I are headed for the shore.

The above examples of lack of parallelism show up in sentences. Business writing calls for two forms of writing that doesn't require complete sentences but do require parallelism. These two areas are bullets and resumes.

Here's an example of lack of parallelism in bullets;

Business writing should be:

- Easy to read
- Easy to understand
- Easy to follow
- Easy to remember
- Contain no grammatical errors

Notice that the first four bullets start with an adjective, ***easy***, but the last one starts with a verb, ***contain***. These bullets are not parallel. You should change the last bullet to read:

- Free from grammatical errors

Now, each bullet starts with an adjective.

When you use bullets, start each bullet with the same part of speech. If you start with a verb in the first bullet, use verbs to start all of your bullets. If you start with nouns, use nouns with each bullet.

Let me share an example of how this works with a resume.

> **Senior Cost/Systems Analyst   March 1987- Present**
>
> - Increased responsibilities resulting from demonstrated proficiency in the use of verbal and analytical skills
>
> - Instruct new employees in various cost and systems procedures
>
> - Chosen to coordinate first-time study at a remote location (International Office - New York)
>
> - Organized and executed project schedule for staff of four over a five-day period
>
> **Cost/Systems Analyst   October 1984 - March 1987**
>
> - Developed and conducted in-depth cost studies for various user areas within the bank
>
> - Identified cost savings and system improvements
>
> - Conduct staff analyses and cite recommendations when warranted
>
> - Served as Variable Budgeting Coordinator/Liaison for Community Banking Division
>
> **New Accounts Advisor   May 1979 - October 1984**
>
> - Opened all accounts within the branch
>
> - Advised potential and current customers on bank services and investments
>
> - Reconciled customer complaints/inquiries on a daily basis
>
> - Office Representative for Branch Automation System Training
>
> - Responsible for cross-training staff in various subsequent phases

Some of you may have noticed that the job titles and lengths of time in the sample resume above were underlined. Yes, I did recommend that you not underline. This sample resume appears with the underlining because that is the way I received it. I did not want to change it for the sake of this book.

In the first section under Senior Cost/System Analyst, notice the first words of the bullets — ***increased, instruct, chosen, organized. Increased,***

Construction Signs That Mean Rough Road Ahead

chosen, and *organized* are verbs in the past tense. *Instruct* is a verb in the present tense. To make that section parallel, you must first change *instruct* to *instructed*. Now all the verbs are in the past tense. However, in that section you need to consider another element. The verb, *chosen*, indeed, is in the past tense. However, it does not describe an action done by the person the resume is about. Somebody else did the choosing, not the person described in the resume.

To change this, you would say:

> *Coordinated first-time study at a remote location (International Office - New York)*

In the second section, did you spot the bullet word that should jump out at you? Right, *conduct*. The other words - *developed*, *identified* and *served* are in the past tense. *Conduct* is in the present tense. So, you need to change it to *conducted*.

The third section would make a professional editor's heart glow. In that section, *opened*, *advised*, and *reconciled* are verbs in the past tense. *Office Representative* is a noun. You can change that to read:

> **Represented the office for Branch Automation System Training**

or

> *Served as the Office Representative for Branch Automation System Training*

The last bullet starts with the adjective, *responsible*. You can change that to read:

> *Cross-trained the staff in various subsequent phases*

Again, now all of the verbs are in the past tense and the section is parallel.

As a reminder, I offer another suggestion concerning the last bullet. Drop the word subsequent and say:

> *Cross-trained the staff in various operational phases*

Avoid Confusing Abbreviations

Sample Confusing Abbreviations		
i.e.	dBA	DOS
e.g.	DBA	RFP
etc.	dba	LCD
et al.	D.B.A.	a.k.a.
op. cit.	f.o.b.	AKA

I am not suggesting that you avoid using abbreviations. Abbreviations serve a useful function in writing. For example, most people clearly understand the meanings of the following abbreviations.

Mr.   **Mrs.**   **Sr.**   **Jr.**

Those four commonly used abbreviations differ greatly from abbreviations that can confuse readers. Either the readers do not know what the abbreviations mean or the writer has used them incorrectly.

The two worst abbreviations you could ever use in a business document are **i.e.** and **e.g.**

Let me explain why. The world is divided into three equal halves concerning those two abbreviations. The first half of the world knows exactly what those two abbreviations mean. The second half of the world does **not** know what those two abbreviations mean and the third half of the world uses them interchangeably. They are not interchangeable.

The abbreviation **i.e.** stands for the latin term *id est*, which means "that is." The abbreviation **e.g.** stands for the latin term *exempli gratia* which means "for example."

You use the abbreviation **i.e.** to indicate something very specific. You use **e.g.** for something that is general and offers examples. When you use **i.e.**, you can only list one item or idea.

Technically, you should use **i.e.** only when that abbreviation is followed by a reference or restatement of the idea or concept that preceded **i.e.** The word, *restatement* is the key word. It means saying the original idea or statement in another way to help the reader understand the writer's intent more clearly.

Construction Signs That Mean Rough Road Ahead

Check out the following example.

He enjoys physical contact sports, i.e., football, hockey and rugby.

This is incorrect because the items that follow **i.e.** are examples and not a restatement of the original idea.

To state that correctly using the abbreviations **i.e.** and **e.g.** you would need to write:

He enjoys physical contact sports, i.e., sports that offer opportunities to "prove" masculinity by inflicting pain or injury to an opponent.

or

He enjoys physical contact sports, e.g., football, hockey and rugby.

I also recommend limited use of other business abbreviations because readers sometimes do not understand what the abbreviations stand for. For example, the abbreviation **f.o.b.**, means different things to different people. The abbreviations **a.k.a**, **dba**, and **et al.** have very specific meanings in certain areas or professions.

Again, not everyone knows or understands what these abbreviations stand for.

If a lawyer sent a document to another lawyer using the abbreviation **dba**, both should understand the abbreviation. If you were to write something in an academic setting, using the abbreviation **et al.** might work. When you leave a strictly legal or academic environment, you risk the chance that your readers might not understand the meanings of those abbreviations.

Acronyms pose another set of problems. Acronyms provide a very useful communication tool when used properly and with common sense.

Let me explain what I mean.

I often ask participants from the banking industry who attend my seminars to tell me what the acronym ATM stands for. You would be amazed at how many people in the banking industry do not know what ATM stands for. The acronym ATM stands for Automated Teller Machine. The problem is many people think it means Automatic Teller Machine or Automatic Transaction Machine.

Still, others are not familiar with this acronym because they use MAC machines.

As I mentioned, acronyms do serve a useful function. Allow me to recommend a technique for using acronyms that should help you and help your readers.

Normally, you would use the phrase, Automated Teller Machine and then, in parenthesis, type the letters ATM. Or, you might type the acronym ATM and then, in parenthesis, insert Automated Teller Machine. Both of these techniques let your readers know what the acronym means.

After doing so, you would then use only the acronym throughout the document.

I recommend that after you use an acronym four times that you once again insert the meaning of the acronym. You might do this after the fourth use or the first time the acronym appears on the following pages.

Be careful to avoid the overuse of acronyms and abbreviations particular to your industry, company, or department when sending documents outside those given areas. For example, if you are in the insurance industry and send documents to customers this becomes increasingly more important.

When in doubt, check it out or leave it out!

Construction Signs That Mean Rough Road Ahead

CHAPTER REVIEW

The following list highlights the more important topics discussed in this chapter. Scan them to see how many you can explain to someone else. If you cannot, I hope you invest the time to review them before moving on to the next section.

Avoid Dang Modifiers

Dang Modifiers refer to phrases or clauses that appear in the wrong places in a sentence. Because of that, they seem to "dangle" off the wrong part of the sentence. For example:

> **Swinging from branch to branch, the little boy enjoyed watching the playful monkey.**

That sentence implies that the little boy was swinging from branch to branch. The sentence should read:

> *The little boy enjoyed watching the playful monkey swing from branch to branch.*

Avoid Needless Words

Let's review this section by talking about three examples.

The first is the phrase, *with respect to*. Rather than using three words you can use one. You can use either ***about***, ***regarding***, or ***concerning***.

For example, review the following sentence.

> **We will contact you in two weeks with respect to the matter of additional payments.**

You can change this sentence to read:

> *We will contact you in two weeks about the matter of additional payments.*
>
> or

> *We will contact you in two weeks about any need for additional payments.*

or

> *We will contact you in two weeks regarding the matter of additional payments.*

or

> *We will contact you in two weeks concerning additional payments.*

Another group of overused needless words are, *I would like to…*

> **I would like to thank you for presenting our group with timely and useful information.**

Rather than just "liking to do it," just do it. Eliminate the phrase, *I would like to,* and say:

> *Thank you for presenting our group with timely and useful information.*

Avoid Clichés

Clichés are phrases that add length but add no strength. And, they can confuse readers, particularly those unfamiliar with the **Clichés** or readers whose primary language is not English.

If you had never heard or read the following expressions, what picture would you paint in your mind after reading them?

> *Hop on the bandwagon*
>
> *Bite the bullet*
>
> *Beat a dead horse*

I think you get the idea. Avoid **Clichés** in business writing.

Construction Signs That Mean Rough Road Ahead

Avoid Jargon

If you were told to "weigh anchor," would you go to the "bow," the "stern," "port" or "starboard" area of a ship?

If you were told, "The suicide squeeze is on. Take the first one, then drag one towards first," what game would you be playing?

Do you know what profession uses the term "anomalous propagation?"

The three sentences above used **Jargon** particular to specific segments of society. In writing, we often use words, phrases or acronyms called **Jargon** to save time or space with internal communication.

Check your writing to ensure you have eliminated references that people "outside" your circle of influence might not understand.

Avoid Incorrect Grammar

Consider these sentences.

> **We was interested in going but now we ain't.**
>
> **When a customer signs up for programs, they need to complete all the forms.**
>
> **A chicken with one leg and a duck was seen walking across the road.**

Each of the above three sentences contains grammatical errors. Grammar checkers should find the errors and suggest ways to correct them.

Errors in grammar are not always as obvious as the first example. For example, consider what I did when I was creating this section. For the explanation above, I wrote:

> **Each of the above three sentences contain grammatical errors.**

Fortunately, my grammar checker caught the mistake and highlighted it in the text and allowed me to correct it. Can you spot what error almost became part of my book?

Avoid Localisms

Localisms are words or phrases that you hear or see in local areas. The problem arises when writers use them in letters, memos, reports or e-mails that leave the local area.

For example, if native "Pittsburghers" were to write a letter to clients in Chicago and use the **Localism**, "Your check needs cashed." The Chicago people might question the intelligence or education of the "Pittsburghers."

The **Helpful Hints** section reminded you to find some friends to help improve your writing. I then extended that hint to include friends who are not from your local area.

They will spot **Localisms** quickly and easily.

Also, your grammar checkers will find most localisms.

Avoid Foreign Phrases

Many people insert **Foreign Phrases** into their writing to impress their audiences. Rather than impressing the audiences, **Foreign Phrases** confuse or frustrate readers. This happens for two reasons. First, the readers may not know the meaning of the foreign word or phrase. This is not good. It wastes time and effort for both the readers and the writers.

Second, writers sometimes use **Foreign Phrases** incorrectly. If the readers know what the **Foreign Phrase** means but the writer uses it incorrectly, the writer looses credibility and results.

Ergo, stay away from **Foreign Phrases.** That includes the word, *ergo*!

Avoid Redundancy

Consider the following sentence.

In the month of June, in the year of 1999, the general consensus of opinion was that the man with a smile on his face, with the color red on his cheeks, was a welcome sight.

Construction Signs That Mean Rough Road Ahead

June is a month.

1999 is a year.

Consensus means opinion.

We find smiles on faces, not on other body parts.

Red is a color.

So, eliminating the **Redundancy** allows us to shorten that sentence to:

In June of 1999, the consensus was that the man with the smile and red cheeks was a welcome sight.

I know! I know! The sentence doesn't make any sense. I simply used the redundant phrases to show how they require you to write more words and delay the message.

The poor sentence with the **Redundancy** used 35 words. The edited version used 20 words.

Why do people like to use **Redundancy?**

100 Words – 10 pages – 2 Blue Books. Big People Like Big Words Big – People Like Big Sentences.

Avoid Polysyllabic Substitutions

A **Polysyllabic Substitution** implies using a word that has more than two syllables for a word that has less than two. This does not mean you should avoid all words with more than two syllables.

The message here is to use shorter, more familiar words that people recognize easily and interpret the same way you mean it. The last sentence contained several words with more than two syllables.

The words *familiar*, *recognize*, *easily*, and *interpret* in that sentence have more than two syllables. However, I believe all of you understood what the sentence meant.

I recommend avoiding words that have more than two syllables if people can interpret the words differently than you mean them.

To test this concept, I asked participants in one of my workshops to give me their interpretations of the following words: *cognizant - conundrum - initiate - initiatives.*

Forty percent did not know what the word *cognizant* meant.

Seventy percent did not know the meaning of *conundrum*. By the way, I predict that word, conundrum, will become the "word of the decade." The word *paradigm* was the "word of the decade" during the 1990s.

In the class, I gave the participants a choice of telling me what the words *initiate* or *initiatives* meant. Let me share some of the answers I got for that question.

> To start – leader
>
> Start something
>
> To propose something new or different
>
> To take action
>
> Choices – make it happen
>
> Right or correct moves
>
> Reasons for doing something
>
> Doing things outside the norm
>
> Goals
>
> Show an interest in working towards a goal
>
> Activities assigned

As you can see, people have different interpretations for the same word. I recommend using shorter more familiar words to save you and the reader time.

Avoid A Preponderance of Prepositional Phrases

The phrase ***avoid a preponderance of prepositional phrases*** contains six words. I could have said, "Avoid needless prepositional phrases." That

Construction Signs That Mean Rough Road Ahead

phrase would only require four words. I used the longer version to show how using too many prepositional phrases results in longer sentences.

The major problem with using too many prepositional phrases goes back to the idea of the **Subject — Verb — Relationship**. The more nouns and pronouns you use in a sentence, the more confused your readers get trying to determine the subject of the sentence.

> **With $5 million in his bank account and a portfolio of valuable stocks, bond and mutual funds, one of the most recognized CEOs of the modern time, Abra Cadabra, Jr., set to rescue yet another company with ROI problems.**

Can you tell me the subject of that sentence? If you can, call me, write me, fax me or email me. I can edit this sentence to 28 words with a clear subject. The original sentence contains 39 words.

Avoid Weighted, Unnatural Language

Many people in business believe they have to write the same way in business as they did in high school or college. They believed that these English teachers really wanted big words and long sentences. Indeed, I have experienced some of these teachers myself. I do not believe all high school and college English teachers call for weighted, unnatural language.

Other business people feel they need to use weighted, unnatural language to impress their bosses or their clients.

Whatever the reasons, I recommend avoiding sentences such as the following.

> **Henceforth, proper procedures need to be followed to bring about a more stabilized and efficient departmental operation.**

What does that mean? It could mean different things to different people. Just say what you mean clearly and concisely. Don't use obscure words or phrases.

What does *stabalized* and *efficient* mean in the sample sentence? What exactly does *departmental operation* mean?

How To Get It Right When You Write

It could mean:

> *We need to follow departmental procedures to ensure proper handling of customer requests.*

Avoid Weak Openings and Weak Closings

Using **Weak Openings and Weak Closings** can send mixed messages to your readers. The first might be that you don't care about the readers. Using **Weak Openings and Weak Closings** could indicate that you don't have time to write them a personal note.

It might also show that you create business documents with a form-letter mentality. Form-letters fall in the same category as "junk mail." The letters all sound alike and look alike because the writers all use the same words and phrases to express the same thing. Using **Weak Openings and Weak Closings** is like hearing someone say, "Last but not least…" Almost everyone uses it so now people are tired of hearing it. The same goes for **Weak Openings and Weak Closings.**

Rather than saying, **Thanking you in advance**, say *Thank you*. Doing so uses two less words. Rather than saying **According to our records** say *Our records show*. Instead of saying **Feel free to call**, say *I will call you to follow up*.

Rather than using phrases everyone sees in business documents all the time, use a more conversational style and personal tone to get better results.

Avoid The Gender Syndrome

The **Gender Syndrome** refers to the use of sexist terms in business writing. The most common example involves using the masculine pronouns – him, he, or his.

To correct the problem of the **Gender Syndrome**, find the bothersome masculine pronouns, determine the antecedent of the pronouns, and then change the antecedent from singular to plural.

Construction Signs That Mean Rough Road Ahead

For example:

Every supervisor must sign the time cards of his workers.

The masculine pronoun in that sentence is *his*. The antecedent – the noun to which the pronoun refers is – *supervisor*.

Pluralizing *supervisor* requires you to pluralize *his* to become *their*. The sentence would then read:

All supervisors must sign the time cards of their workers.

Avoid Negative Tone

Tell your readers what you can or will do for them, not what you can't or won't. Tell your readers what they can or should do.

Positive sentences generally create positive results.

Please don't hesitate to call

becomes

Please call me.

Our meeting shouldn't last more than two hours

becomes

Our meeting will last less than two hours

Avoid Abstract and Non-specific Terms

One of your goals as a writer is to paint pictures for your readers. Successful writing means that the readers see the same pictures that writers intend. **Abstract and Non-specific Terms** do not paint clear pictures.

In many instances, **Abstract and Non-specific Terms** end in "ion, or tion." Consider the following sentence.

If you complete the following form, you will win a fabulous vacation.

The key word in that sentence is *vacation*. Different people see their vacations differently. If the fabulous *vacation* advertised were a trip to Hawaii, people who are allergic to sand and sun might not think it's fabulous.

If the highlight of the *vacation* was a trip to the top of the Washington Monument and the winner were afraid of heights, the *vacation* might not be as appealing.

Avoid Lack of Parallelism

Lack of parallelism occurs in sentence form or in bullets. In sentence form, we use the example, **I like hunting, fishing, and to go swimming**. The correct sentence would read:

I like hunting, fishing, and swimming.

In bullet form, we reviewed the following example using bullets:

- Easy to read
- Easy to understand
- Easy to follow
- Easy to remember
- Contain no grammatical errors

To correct that list, change the last bullet to read:

- **Free from grammatical errors**

Now each bullet begins with an adjective.

Avoid Confusing Abbreviations

Abbreviations serve a useful function in writing because they can save us time and space. This chapter talked about avoiding **Confusing Abbreviations**.

Confusing Abbreviations fall into several catagories.

Construction Signs That Mean Rough Road Ahead

Foreign phrases:
- i.e.
- e.g.
- etc.

Legal abbreviations:
- DBA
- et al.
- Ad Manum

Educational abbreviations:
- op. cit.
- ibid
- idem

Departmental abbreviations:
- SOF
- RFP
- SOW

Industry specific:
- ABS
- LCD
- DOS

The major message when using abbreviations is to focus on your audience. If you are 110% sure your audience knows and understands the abbreviations the way you mean them, use them. If the abbreviations fall into the catagories listed above, think twice about using them.

"Avoid words and phrases that add length but no strength."

Chapter Five
Reality Check

Congratulations. If you read this entire book, completed the practice activities, and compared your approach to the suggestions that followed each activity, you should begin to see an immediate improvement in your business writing.

This chapter is your reality check. To ensure you really own the concepts in this book, use this chapter to determine what ideas really stuck.

Glance at the chapter-by-chapter reviews that follow and try to remember the explanations for each section. Pretend a friend asked you to explain a specific section or idea.

For example, how would you tell a friend the difference between the **Active** and **Passive Voice**? Could you give your friend three ways to spot the passive voice and two ways to change it into the **Active Voice**? If not, review the section to see how using the **Active Voice** helps you become clear and concise. Remember how using your grammar checkers to find the **Passive Voice** will save you time.

Let's begin reviewing.

Chapter One • You Win – Guaranteed
Seven Reasons Why You Should Read This Book

Reason #1   This book works - guaranteed.

Reason #2   You will learn these techniques easily and apply them immediately.

Reason #3   You will gain a personal business writing coach.

Reason #4   You will learn the reasons *why* these techniques work and *how* they will improve your writing, your attitude and your income.

Reason #5 You will practice what you learn and get immediate feedback to check your progress.

Reason #6 You will learn from real-life business situations and writing samples.

Reason #7 You will find this book easy to read and apply.

Will This Book Meet Your Objectives?

Yes, I Want To

- ❏ **Save time**
- ❏ **Get better results**
- ❏ **Become clear and concise**
- ❏ **Set the proper tone**
- ❏ **Make more money**
- ❏ **Improve my personal and corporate image**
- ❏ **Eliminate fear and dread of writing**
- ❏ **Reduce stress and frustration**
- ❏ **Make my readers think I am brilliant**
- ❏ **Focus on my audience**
- ❏ **Check my writing for quality**
- ❏ **Flush out** *fony frazes*
- ❏ **Build confidence in my writing**
- ❏ **Write in a conversational manner**
- ❏ **Create exciting writing**

Reality Check

Stop! You just passed an opportunity to create an **Action Plan**. Now that you have completed the book, what do you plan to work on? Go back to the objectives on the previous page and check at least three items and then create a plan for how you intend to meet those objectives.

Or, use the white space below to write down three ideas you picked up from the book that you would like to work on to make your writing tasks easier or to help you get better results.

Chapter 2 • Fire! Ready! Aim!

Five Things You Must Know Before You Write

1. Your business writing is a valuable corporate asset. People decide important business issues based on what you write.

2. The biggest time waster in business writing is spending too much time in the **Writing Stage** and not enough in the **Prewriting** and **Editing Stages**. Remember your high school term paper? You spent more time researching and editing than you did writing.

3. People fear and dread writing because they remember focusing on **100 Words - 10 Pages - 2 Blue books**. They convinced themselves **that big people like big words and big people like big sentences**. They filled their documents with long sentences that used big words and unnecessary prepositional phrases.

4. **Communication means caring and sharing**. It means caring enough about your audience to write in a way that people understand your words the way you mean them. More than half of all communication takes place nonverbally. When we write, we do not have the benefit of nonverbal messages. That's why writing is so tough. We must rely on the words and the tone when we write.

5. The term **Speed Traps** refers to the fact that we think a lot faster than we write or read. Only a small portion of the information our mind processes each minute relates to our writing topic. The rest pertains to other facets of our business and personal life. That means as we write, we compete with everything else going on in our business and personal life. And, we compete with the business and personal lives of our readers.

That's a lot of competition for us as we write and for our readers as they read.

Seven Helpful Hints

1. Write to be understood, not to overwhelm.
2. Become intimate with your grammar checkers.
3. Average 18 words per sentence.
4. Find some friends.
5. Use a 24-hour drawer.
6. Read your writing out loud.
7. Proofread, proofread, proofread.

Yes, You Can

- End a sentence with a preposition.
- Start a sentence with *because*.
- Use the same word twice in a sentence.
- Begin a sentence with *but, and, nor,* or *or*.

Reality Check

- Use one sentence paragraphs.
- Use contractions.
- Split infinitives.
- Save the Topic Sentence for the last thing you write.
- Begin a sentence with "I".
- Use "I" in business letters.

Subject - Verb - Relationship

The **Subject - Verb - Relationship** is really the key to good writing. Paying attention to it keeps your writing clear and concise.

Remember these sentences that explained the **Subject - Verb - Relationship**?

The dog bit the man.

The man bit the dog.

These sentences contain the same words. The arrangement of those words in the **Subject - Verb - Relationship** determines the picture your mind receives when you read the words.

In the first sentence, *dog* serves as the subject and *man* shows the relationship. In the second sentence, the **Subject - Verb - Relationship** changes so that *man* becomes the subject and *dog* shows the relationship.

Remember, in business, people want to know who is doing what or what is doing what. You express that information in the **Subject - Verb - Relationship**. Forget the descriptive adjectives, fluffy adverbs, and big words. Focus on making the **Subject - Verb - Relationship** clear, specific and accurate.

Chapter 3 • Mommy and Daddy Need To Party

This chapter showed you five ways incorrect verbs and verb constructions destroy good writing.

Avoid Weak Verbs

Weak Verbs force you to use more words and often weakens the **Subject - Verb - Relationship**. Remember this partial list of Weak Verbs?

Am	Have	Make
Are	Has	Take
Is	Had	Give
Was		
Were	Do	
Be	Did	
Been	Done	

I had an enjoyable time at your party.

becomes

I enjoyed your party.

Avoid Passive Voice

You find the **Passive Voice** when:

- a **Weak Verb** helps a **Strong Verb**, and
- the subject of the sentence is not performing the action of the verb and
- the person or thing performing the action shows up at the end of the sentence as an object of the preposition. Sometimes, the person or thing performing the action never shows up.

The beer was sipped by Jake.

In this sentence, the **Weak Verb**, *was*, appears with the **Strong Verb**, *sipped*.

The *beer* is not the person or thing performing the action of the verb. The person performing the action, *Jake*, appears as the object of a preposition at the end of the sentence.

To improve the sentence, you would write:

Jake sipped the beer.

Reality Check

Use the **Passive Voice** when:

1. The Doer of the action is not known.

   The bomb was mysteriously placed in the airport locker.

2. The Doer of the action is not important.

   He was elected by only three votes.

3. You want to be extremely sensitive or do not want to reveal something.

   A mistake was made in adding the figures.

4. You use the Passive Voice in a subordinate clause.

   Use the Passive Voice when the Doer of the action is not known.

Avoid Nowhere Adverbs

Nowhere Adverbs are those constructions in American business writing that start with the adverb, *there* and add a **Weak Verb**. For example, *there are*, *there is*, *there could have been*, *there should have been*.

Nowhere Adverbs:

- Force you to use Weak Verbs.
- Cloud the Subject.
- Add no value or impact to the sentence.
- Force you to use longer sentences.

   There are many things you must learn before you are promoted.

   becomes

   You must learn many things before you are promoted.

   or

   You must learn many things before I promote you.

Avoid Artificial Antecedents

You might remember this as the *It Thing*.

Artificial Antecedents start with the pronoun *it* and add a **Weak Verb** or the **Passive Voice** to create a construction that makes a sentence longer, more confusing and less personal.

If the sentence begins with an **Artificial Antecedent**, *it* becomes the subject of the sentence. When that happens, we do not know who or what is doing the action. That's where confusion sets in.

> **It is obvious that the Hinkle Dinkle Manufacturing Company hires the best people.**

becomes

> *The Hinkle Dinkle Manufacturing Company hires the best people.*

Avoid Turning Strong Verbs Into Nouns or Adjectives

Verbs become nouns by adding *ion, tion, ation, al, ment, sis* or *ive* onto a strong verb.

> **Our manager made a recommendation that we sell the returned goods for half price.**

In the sentence above, the writer weakened the **Strong Verb** *recommend* by adding *ation* to the end of it to make it a noun. This also made the sentence a lie because the manager did not *make* anything. And, turning the **Strong Verb** into a noun created a longer sentence.

The sentence should read:

> *Our manager recommended that we sell the returned goods for half price.*

Time Saving Bonus

Under the Time-saving Bonus section, you found these three ideas.

1. Use your grammar checkers to help you find common errors in writing.

2. Use the **Edit** feature of your word processing package.
3. Keep a list of words or phrases that you might commonly misuse so you can run them through the **Edit** feature.

Chapter 4 • Construction Signs That Mean Rough Road Ahead

Let's review other constructions that create longer sentences, confuse the readers and thus, weaken your writing.

The following list describes constructions that you should avoid in writing.

Avoid Dang Modifiers

If there is an Al Borowski in the building, please report to the main lobby.

becomes

Al Borowski, please report to the lobby.

Avoid Needless Words

The purpose of this memo is to provide information with respect to the subject of overtime abuses.

becomes

This memo provides information on overtime abuses.

Avoid Clichés

Last but not least, I am more than happy to introduce this man with the smile on his face, who will grease the skids for us this morning.

That sentence contains four clichés.

Last but not least
More than happy
Smile on his face
Grease the skids

Avoid Jargon

Remember that **Jargon** refers to words, phrases or acronyms we use in speech and writing to save time or space with internal communication. The important phrase is *internal communication*. When you write to employees or customers who do not understand the expressions, you risk miscommunication.

For example, can you interpret this "jargon-filled" sentence from the insurance industry?

> **Even with an endorsement, we cannot offer full tort on your universal life.**

Avoid Incorrect Grammar

> **Between you and I**

becomes

> *Between you and me*

> **For you and I**

becomes

> *For you and me*

> **Where are you at?**

becomes

> *Where are you?*

> **Where are you going to?**

becomes

> *Where are you going?*

Each of the above three sentences contain grammatical errors.

becomes

Each of the above three sentences contains grammatical errors.

Use the grammar checker built into your word processing software. If the software package does not include a grammar checker, I recommend investing in a stand-alone version of one. It will save you time and embarrassment.

Grammar checkers are not perfect. But, they are a big help.

Avoid Localisms

Localisms are words or phrases that you hear or see in local areas. The problem arises when writers use them in letters, memos, reports or e-mails that leave the local area.

For some reason, "Pittsburghers" overuse the word *whenever* and seldom use the word *when*.

When is an adverb that indicates a *specific* time. **Whenever** is a conjunction that indicates an event can happen *any* time or *every* time.

For example:

When the cow jumped over the moon, the dish ran away with the spoon.

That sentence indicates a specific point in time when the dish ran away. Thus, you would use ***when***.

But if you said:

Whenever the cow jumped over the moon, the dish ran away with the spoon.

This sentence implies that the cow *had jumped* many times and might do it again. The sentence did not indicate a ***specific*** time that the cow jumped but implies that *anytime* it happened, the dish would run.

I clearly remember having explained this in one of my workshops just before we took a break. During the break, one of the participants said to another, "Whenever I got out of the service, I started looking for a job." Think about that. How many times was this guy in the service?

Using the word *whenever* implied he had done this or will do this more than once. I suspect he was discharged from the military only once, and thus, that was a specific event. So he should have said, "When I got out of the service, I started looking for a new job."

Another localisms I hear in Pittsburgh is the word *slippy*.

"Pittsburghers" will say:

> **The dusting of snow made the sidewalks slippy.**

The correct word is **slippery**.

> ***The dusting of snow made the sidewalks slippery.***

Please forgive me for using so many Pittsburgh localisms. Because I live in Pittsburgh, I hear a lot of them and am more familiar with them.

As I recommended, ask friends who are not originally from your local area to read your writing. They will find the localisms you use.

Avoid Foreign Phrases

English is tough enough the way it is. Don't try to impress your readers by using foreign phrases.

Doing so can confuse readers who do not know the English translation of the phrase. Or, doing so can lessen your chances of success if your readers have a different interpretation of the phrases you use. Or, you may use the wrong foreign phrase or use one incorrectly. Don't take chances with your writing by using foreign phrases.

Reality Check

Voila. Your caveat proved to be a faux pas.

I won't even try to translate that for you!

Avoid Redundancy

Redundancy means saying the same thing twice, two different ways.

One of the best examples of redundancy is the very unique phrase "close proximity."

One of the best is incorrect because you can only have one person or thing that is *the best*.

You should not use a word like *very*, which is used to compare items, with a phrase that means *one of a kind*. You have nothing to compare it to.

And, *close* and *proximity* mean the same thing.

Avoid Polysyllabic Substitutions

Polysyllabic means having more than two syllables. Use shorter familiar words so your readers need not scramble to find a dictionary to understand what you mean.

Forcing your readers to find words in a dictionary wastes their time and risks unsatisfactory results.

I must reiterate that to utilize remuneration to mitigate the circumstances could initiate an endeavor to execute an altercation.

If that example were a real sentence, it might mean something like:

I must repeat that using money to smooth over the situation could create an attempt to start a fight.

Even that sentence says too much. The point here is simple. Use shorter, more familiar words to clearly state an idea rather than fancy, big words to impress your readers. Trust me. They are not impressed.

Avoid A Preponderance of Prepositional Phrases

The more you can focus on the **Subject-Verb-Relationship**, the clearer your writing becomes. Limiting the number of prepositional phrases means you have less chance to bury what should be the subject of the sentence as the object of a preposition.

> **Men of medicine generally manifest a predilection for an apparatus known in their esoteric nomenclature as a sphygmomanometer for the purpose of determining the systolic and diastolic parameters of their clientele in an effort to ascertain their degree of wellness.**

becomes

> *Doctors prefer to use an instrument called a sphygmomanometer to test their patients' blood pressure.*

Avoid Weighted, Unnatural Language

Remember what Lee Iacocca said. "If you don't think that way, don't write that way."

> **The following are some of the problems which were instrumental in contributing to the dissolution of the program.**

I believe Mr. Iacocca would have said:

> *I canceled the program because...*

or

> *The program failed because...*

Avoid Weak Openings and Weak Closings

Weak openings and weak closings signal a lazy, form-letter, impersonal approach to writing. All three approaches lessen your chances of getting the results you want.

> *Per your request, enclosed please find the aforementioned.*

If you review any part of the book, please review the section on Weak Openings and Weak Closings. I ask that you do that because the phrases listed in that section are overused because of habit. To gain the most from this book, you need to break some of your writing habits.

Avoid The Gender Syndrome

The Gender Syndrome refers to the use of sexist terms in business writing.

> **The creative writer does not wait for chance to bring *him* inspiration, *he* develops *his* own.**

To correct the Gender Syndrome, first, find the bothersome masculine pronouns. In the above example, they are ***him***, ***he*** and ***his***. Then, pluralize their antecedents. In the example, the antecedent for all three is ***writer***. That becomes ***writers***. That means you must also use the plural form of the verb. So, ***does*** becomes ***do***.

The sentence now becomes:

> *Creative writers do not wait for chance to bring them inspiration; they develop their own.*

Avoid Negative Tone

Tell your readers what you can or will do for them, not what you can't or won't do. Tell your readers what they can or should do, not what they can't do.

Simply put, you will get better results with a positive tone.

> **I won't be in my office until June 3rd.**

becomes

> *I will be in my office June 3rd.*

or

> *I will return to my office June 3rd.*

Avoid Abstract and Non-specific Terms

This means you should use words that create clear, graphic, specific mental pictures for your readers. Your readers need to see the same picture you see.

> **The function will feature participatory activities.**

becomes

> *The company picnic will feature a softball game and egg-throwing contests.*

Avoid Lack of Parallelism

To review this concept, let me share with you the example you saw earlier.

Business writing should be:
- ❏ Easy to read
- ❏ Easy to understand

How To Get It Right When You Write

- ❏ Easy to follow
- ❏ Easy to remember
- ❏ Contain no grammatical errors

Notice that the first four bullets start with an adjective, *easy*, but the last one starts with a verb, *contain*. These bullets are not parallel. You should change the last bullet to read:

- ❏ Free from grammatical errors

Now, each bullets starts with an adjective.

When you use bullets, start each bullet with the same part of speech. If you start with a verb in the first bullet, use verbs to start all of your bullets. If you start with nouns, use nouns with each bullet.

Avoid Confusing Abbreviations

Remember, not everyone knows or understands many abbreviations we use in business writing.

Many of the abbreviations we use come from the academic world, from specific business segments such as the legal profession, or as a shortened version of a foreign phrase.

Consider the following abbreviations.

POE	c.o.d.	OEM
Esq.	RAM	pt.
op.cit.	non seq.	Bbl.
ibid.	Loc.	Cit. Idem

If you know the meanings of each of the above listed abbreviations, I congratulate you. If you don't, you can understand why I recommend that you carefully consider using abbreviations in your writing.

As I stated in the text of Chapter Four, when in doubt, check it out or leave it out! Take a quick, informal poll of your audience. Check out whether they understand the abbreviations the way you mean to use them. You might be surprised.

Reality Check

Congratulations and Thank You

How well do you remember the concepts we covered in this book? The more you review the examples and explanations, the easier writing and editing will become for you.

Few people can remember every detail about books they read. For you to gain the most value from this book, you need to glance at the material on a regular basis to recall ideas that can benefit you. You need to create and use a personal Action Plan to focus on specific areas of improvement.

The more you use the concepts, the more valuable the techniques become for helping you with your writing.

As I stated early in the book, if you have any questions, comments, or criticisms, call me; write me; fax me, or e-mail me.

> Al Borowski, MEd, CSP
> Priority Communication Skills, Inc.
> P.O. Box 24505
> Pittsburgh, PA 15234
> Office: 412-561-7628
> Toll Free: 1-877-902-3314
> Fax: 412-561-7035
> E-mail: al@alborowski.com

And please, visit my website at www.alborowski.com. It features articles on writing and other communication topics.

Thank you for buying the book. I hope we meet some day to discuss if and how the book helped you.

Index

A

abbreviations vi, 166, 167, 168, 178, 179, 196
ACS Styles Guide: A Manual for Authors and Ed 71
abstract and Non-specific Terms vi, 161, 177, 195
Action Plan v, 4, 11, 183, 197
active voice 68, 69, 70, 71, 73, 98, 121, 181
adjectives v, 21, 41, 110, 112, 116, 117, 121, 162, 185, 188
Alexandra 58, 154, 155
AMA Style Guide for Business Writing 71, 72
American Chemical Society 71, 72
American Management Association 71, 72, 207
antecedents 94
Art of Readable Writing 31
artificial antecedents 94, 96, 101, 105, 117, 188
as you are aware 148, 152
at this point in time 128, 129
auxiliary verbs 55

B

basic fundamentals 138
Bau, Mary D.Ed viii
become clear and concise 5, 11, 160, 181, 182
begin a sentence with "I" 37, 45, 185
Beverly Hillbillies 143
body language 13, 22
Booth, Carol Baker vii
Borowski, Al, MEd, CSP 2, 197
(Borowski), Brian vii, 81, 82, 161
(Borowski), Marylou vii
build confidence in my writing 9
bullets 163, 164, 178, 196
business writing style guide 35
by and large 130, 132

Index

C

Calore, Pam vii
Calvin 59, 60
Cathy Marie vii, 7, 118, 119
Christine Marie vii, 58
Clampett, Jed 143
clichés vi, 130, 131, 132, 136, 138, 170, 189
close proximity 138, 139, 193
colloquial 134, 144
commence 141, 143
communication process 19
complete 13
complex sentence 16, 88
compound sentence 16
compound-complex sentence 16
confidence vii, 9, 11, 118, 131, 182
continue to occur 138
contractions 35, 36, 45, 92, 185
conundrum 141, 143, 174
conversational manner 9
conversational tone 4
cool as a cucumber 130, 131
coup de grace 136, 137
Cronkite, Walter 34

D

"dang" modifiers 123, 125
dangling modifiers 123
dangling participles 123
declarative 15, 18, 148
demonstrate 121, 141, 142, 164
dependent clause 16
Derek 58
DeVito, Danny 109
diagramming of sentences 49
Douglas, Michael 109

E

editing process 15, 19
editing stage 15
Elements of Style, Strunk and White 70

Index

eliminate fear and dread of writing 7, 182
Emmerling, Ernie viii
enclosed please find 148, 149, 194
end result 138
exact same 138
exclamatory 15, 148
eye contact 22

F

faux pas 136, 193
fear and dread 7, 11, 15, 23, 44, 182, 183
feel free to call 148, 152, 153, 176
find some friends 27
Flesch, Rudolph 31
fony frazes 9, 11, 182
foreign Phrases vi, 136, 137, 172, 179, 192
free of charge 138, 139
Fries, C.C. 31
future prospects 138

G

Galina 20
gender syndrome vi, 157, 176, 194, 195
get better results 5, 11, 13, 18, 31, 156, 158, 176, 182, 183, 195
grammar checkers 26, 29, 30, 37, 44, 48, 49, 67, 74, 101, 117, 119, 121, 125, 171, 172, 181, 184, 188, 189, 220
Grammy (Marylou Borowski) 154
Grampy (Al Borowski) 58, 155
Gregg Reference Manual 31, 70, 156

H

helping verbs 55
Holleran, Diane viii

I

Iacocca, Lee 25, 26, 47, 194
Ian 57
imperative 15, 103, 148, 149
implement 126, 141, 144
improve my personal and corporate image 6, 11, 182

Index

in lieu of 136, 137
in the amount of 128, 129
indent 17
independent clause 16, 74
infinitives 36, 37, 45, 185
interrogative 15, 18, 148
it thing 94, 101, 140, 188

J

jargon vi, 132, 133, 171, 190
Jewel of the Nile 109

L

last but not least 130, 131, 176, 189
left justified 17
linking verbs 47, 59, 60
Localisms vi, 134, 135, 136, 172, 191, 192
long sentences 16, 27, 175, 183
Lydia 87, 89, 90

M

main clause 74
make more money 6,7, 11, 63, 182
make my readers think I am brilliant 8, 182
Marylou 58
mental outlining 25
Mercer, Kim viii
more than happy 130, 132, 189
more than willing 130, 132
Murray, Maureen viii

N

National Council of Teachers of English 31
National Speakers Association viii
needless to say 128, 129
negative tone viii, 5, 35, 100, 152, 154, 158, 159, 160, 177, 195
nonverbal 21, 22, 23, 184
nor 2, 34, 45, 127, 142, 184
nowhere adverbs v, 80, 82, 83, 84, 86, 87, 93, 116, 117, 121, 187

Index

O

outlining format 33

P

paradigm 19, 20, 21, 25, 141, 174
paragraph 16, 17, 33, 37, 54, 71, 127, 128, 140, 151
parallel 162, 163, 165, 196
parallelism viii, 162, 163, 178, 195
past history 138
Pennsylvania Speakers Association viii
Per Se 136
per your request 3, 9, 25, 119, 148, 155, 156, 194
Plain Letter, Federal Stock Number 7610-00-1091 71
please be advised 148, 149
please don't hesitate to call 153, 154, 155, 158, 177
polysyllabic substitutions vi, 141, 166, 173, 193
prepositional phrases vi, 18, 49, 50, 51, 52, 53, 145, 174, 175, 183, 193
pressed into service 130
prewriting 13, 14, 28, 183
prewriting stage 14
prior experience 138
prior record 138, 139
prioritize 141, 143, 144
Priority Communication Skills, Inc. 2, 197
pronouns 38, 49, 94, 148, 157, 175, 176, 195
proofreading 14, 30
proposal 22, 27, 33, 110, 160
Publication Manual of the American Psychological Association 70

Q

quality 8, 11, 26, 37, 182
Qubein, Nido, CSP, CPAE viii

R

reduce stress and frustration 7
redundancy vi, 137, 172, 173, 193,
reiterate 142
repeat again 138
replace 64, 137, 117, 119, 141

Index

report 9, 22, 33, 82, 87, 90, 92, 93, 96, 98, 99, 104, 105, 110, 189
root causes 138
Rule 1080 31

S

Samantha 75, 76
save time 4, 11, 7, 13, 18, 20, 47, 49, 66, 132, 140, 142, 171, 182, 190
Scannell, Ed, CMP, CSP viii
set the proper tone 5, 182
sharing 22, 156, 184
simple sentence 16, 88
speed traps 23, 29, 44, 184
spell checker 29, 119, 129
state of being verbs 47, 59, 60
stress and frustration 11, 182
strong verbs v, 56, 58, 59, 61, 71, 110, 112, 113, 116, 121, 188
Strunk and White 70
Subject - Verb - Relationship 41
subsequently 144

T

talking straight 25
term paper 14, 17, 183
that are designed to 128, 129
the above mentioned 148, 150, 151
the aforementioned 148, 150, 151, 194
time saving bonus v, 117, 119
Topic Sentence 37
Tracy, Brian, CPAE viii
transpire 141, 143
true fact 138
Turner, Kathleen 109

U

up to snuff 130, 132

V

Van Hooser, Phillip viii
Van Hooser, Susan viii
verbal 21, 132, 164

Index

very unique 138, 139, 193
voila 136, 137, 138, 193

W

we regret to inform you 6, 148, 152, 158
weak closings vii, 3, 147, 148, 156, 176, 194
weak openings vi, 3, 147, 148, 156, 176, 194
Wegley, Diane vi
word processing program 117
Writers PEG (Professional Experts Group) of NSA viii
writing stage 14, 15, 28, 44, 183

X

Xerox copies 138

Y

Yes, You Can v, 30, 31, 33, 34, 35, 36, 37, 38, 45, 74, 94, 184

About the author

Al Borowski, MEd, CSP

Al Borowski works with companies who want their employees to communicate clearly and with business professionals who want more impact in their presentations. He helps people save time, reduce stress and get better results when they speak, write or listen. Al has trained more than 10,000 participants as a seminar leader for *The American Management Association, Dun & Bradstreet, Penn State University, The University of Pittsburgh-Katz Graduate School of Business, and Robert Morris College.*

He brings more than twenty years of communication experience to his action-packed keynote speeches, breakout sessions, and workshops. His exciting, innovative approach draws on years of practical application as a sales manager, business development manager, and customer service manager. His background also includes four years as an English teacher. He is a published author and professional musician.

Al is a member of the National Speakers Association, where he received their highest earned designation, CSP (**Certified Speaking Professional**). He is also a Past President of The Pennsylvania Speakers Association and a past board member of the Pittsburgh Chapter of the American Society for Training and Development. He holds a Master's Degree in Adult Education and a certificate in Human Resource Development.

Contact Al at:

Al Borowski, MEd, CSP
Certified Speaking Professional
Priority Communication Skills, Inc.
P.O. Box 24505
Pittsburgh, PA 15234

Phone 412-561-7628
Toll Free 1-877-902-3314
Fax 412-561-7035
E-mail al@alborowski.com
www.alborowski.com

You can bring Al into your organization to conduct one or two-day workshops based on this book.
or,
for your next convention, conference, meeting, or retreat, you can bring Al in to deliver a keynote speech or breakout session.

For availability and topics, contact Al at:

Priority Communication Skills, Inc.
P.O. Box 24505
Pittsburgh, PA 15234
Phone: 412-561-7628
Toll Free: 1-877-902-3314
Fax: 412-561-7035
E-mail: al@alborowski.com
www.alborowski.com

Please fax me your comments on this book using the form on the other side of this page.

Comments Form

Hey Al,

You asked for comments on your book. So, here goes...

_____
_____
_____
_____
_____
_____
_____
_____
_____
_____
_____
_____
_____
_____

I bought your book:
- ❏ at one of your presentations
- ❏ from your website
- ❏ from an e-commerce site (which one) _____
- ❏ from a book store (which one) _____

Name _____ Title _____
Company _____
Address _____
City _____ State _____ Zip _____
Phone _____ Fax _____
E-mail address _____ Website _____

This contact information is for our records only.
We faithfully promise not to share your contact information with anyone.

Please fax this form to 412-561-7035.

Thank You.

Availability Form

Al, please let me know when the following items are available.

Books
❏ How To Get It Right When You Write - Book Two - The Writing Process

E-Book
❏ How to Get It Right When You Write - Book One - The Editing Process

❏ How To Get It Right When You Write - Book Two - The Writing Process

CD's
❏ How to Get It Right When You Write - Book One - The Editing Process

❏ How To Get It Right When You Write - Book Two - The Writing Process

Audio Tapes
❏ How to Get It Right When You Write - Book One - The Editing Process

❏ How To Get It Right When You Write - Book Two - The Writing Process

Special Reports
❏ How to Get It Right When You Write E-mails
   A Standards Manual for Creating Effective E-mails

Name _____ Title _____
Company _____
Address _____
City _____ State _____ Zip _____
Phone _____ Fax _____
E-mail address _____ Website _____

This contact information is for our records only.
We faithfully promise not to share your contact information with anyone.

Please fax this form to 412-561-7035.

Thank You.

ORDER FORM
Share this book with your family, friends, and co-workers.
Order multiple copies and save.

Pricing
 1 - 10 copies $19.95 US each
 11 - 25 copies $17.95 US each
 26 - 50 copies $15.95 US each
 50+ copies Please call us at 1-877-902-3314

To order additional copies of **How to Get it Right When You Write**, please complete the form below and mail with a check, purchase order or credit card information to:

Priority Communication Skills, Inc.
P.O. Box 24505 • Pittsburgh, PA 15234

SHIP TO:	**BILL TO:**
Name	Name
Title	Title
Company	Company
Address	Address
City/State/Zip	City/State/Zip
Phone Fax	Phone Fax
E-mail Address Website	E-mail Address Website

PLEASE SHIP:

QUANTITY	PRICE EACH	TOTAL
PA sales tax 6% except Allegheny County which is 7%		
Add $3.00 for single book orders and $6.00 for each 12 books ordered		
Tax Exempt Number:		
	TOTAL	$

METHOD OF PAYMENT

☐ Check   ☐ Money Order
☐ Visa   ☐ MasterCard

Make check or money order payable to:
Priority Communication Skills, Inc.

Credit Card Number

Expiration Date

Signature

Thank You
For more information call us at 1-877-902-3314